Welcome to *Write Source*!

This *Write Source* book was written just for you. We hope you have fun and learn, too.

Enjoy writing,
Your friends at Write Source

Using the *Write Source* Book

Your *Write Source* book includes lessons and tips about writing. You will learn to write letters, reports, stories, poems, and more.

Besides writing, you will learn how to listen, speak, and take tests in class. Finally, a special section, called the "Proofreader's Guide," explains the rules of writing.

HOUGHTON MIFFLIN HARCOURT

WRITE SOURCE

Authors
Dave Kemper, Patricia Reigel, and Patrick Sebranek

Illustrator
Chris Krenzke

GREAT SOURCE®

HOUGHTON MIFFLIN HARCOURT

Reviewers

Genevieve Bodnar NBCT
Youngstown City Schools
Youngstown, Ohio

Daniel Bower
Blackbird Elementary
Harbor Springs, Michigan

Kay E. Dooley
East Maine School District 63
Des Plaines, Illinois

Mary M. Fischer
Arlington Public Schools
Arlington, Massachusetts

Cynthia Fontenot
Green T. Linden Elementary
Lafayette, Louisiana

Marsha Ganz
School Board of Broward County
Ft. Lauderdale, Florida

Tracey Leatherwood
St. Charles Boromeo School
New York, New York

Lynn A. Lein
Goffstown SAU19
Goffstown, New Hampshire

Lynn Sholes
Broward County Schools
Ft. Lauderdale, Florida

Renee Wiley
P.S. 309
Brooklyn, New York

WRITE SOURCE Online
www.hmheducation.com/writesource

Printed in the U.S.A.

ISBN 978-0-547-48489-1

6 7 8 9 10 0868 1 9 18 17 16 15 14

4500488055 A B C D E F G

Quick Guide

Contents

The Process of Writing

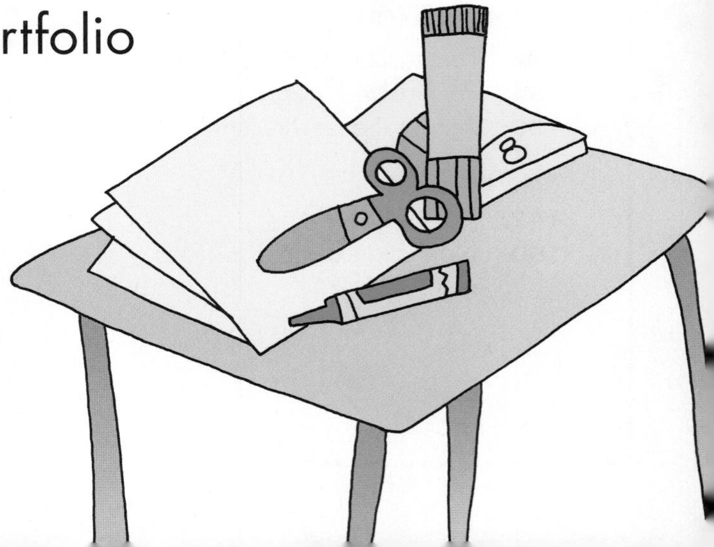

The Tools of Learning

Words

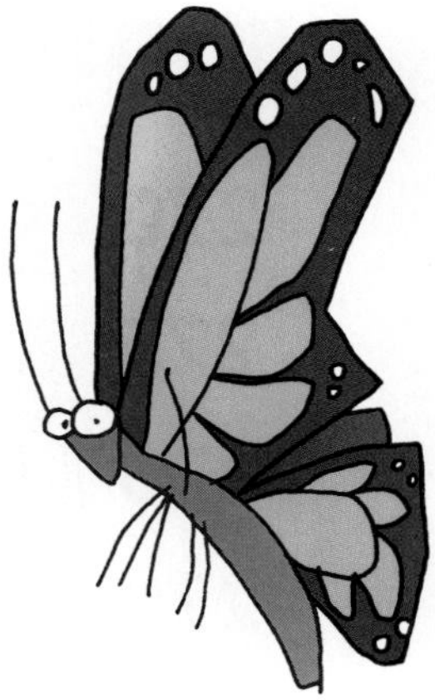

A Writer's Resource

Proofreader's Guide

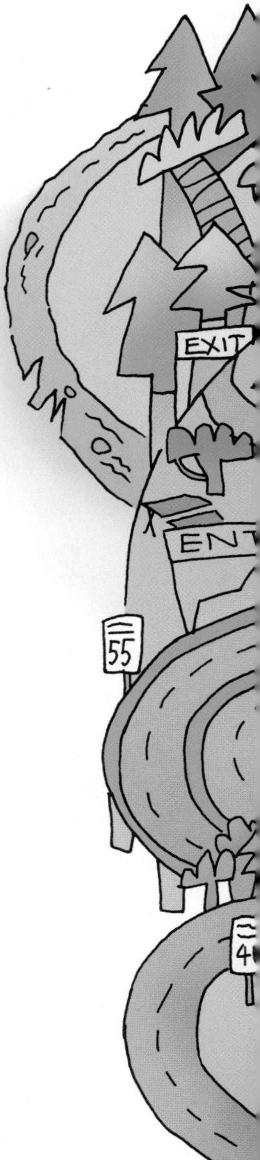

Theme Words

Why Write?

You write to share your thoughts and feelings with other people. Sometimes you write just for yourself.

Writing will help you . . .

- **share with others.** You can write notes, cards, letters, and e-mail messages to family and friends.
- **remember more.** You can write down interesting facts and make reports.
- **learn more about yourself.** You can write about your thoughts and feelings.
- **have fun.** You can write poems, stories, and jokes.

The Writing Process

Academic Vocabulary

Work with a partner. Read the meanings and share answers to the questions.

1. When you **plan** something, you make up your mind about what you are going to do and how you will do it.
   How would you plan a picnic?
2. The **main** thing is the most important one.
   What is the main thing you bring to school everyday?

There are five steps in the writing process: prewrite, write, revise, edit, and publish. You can use these steps to help you write.

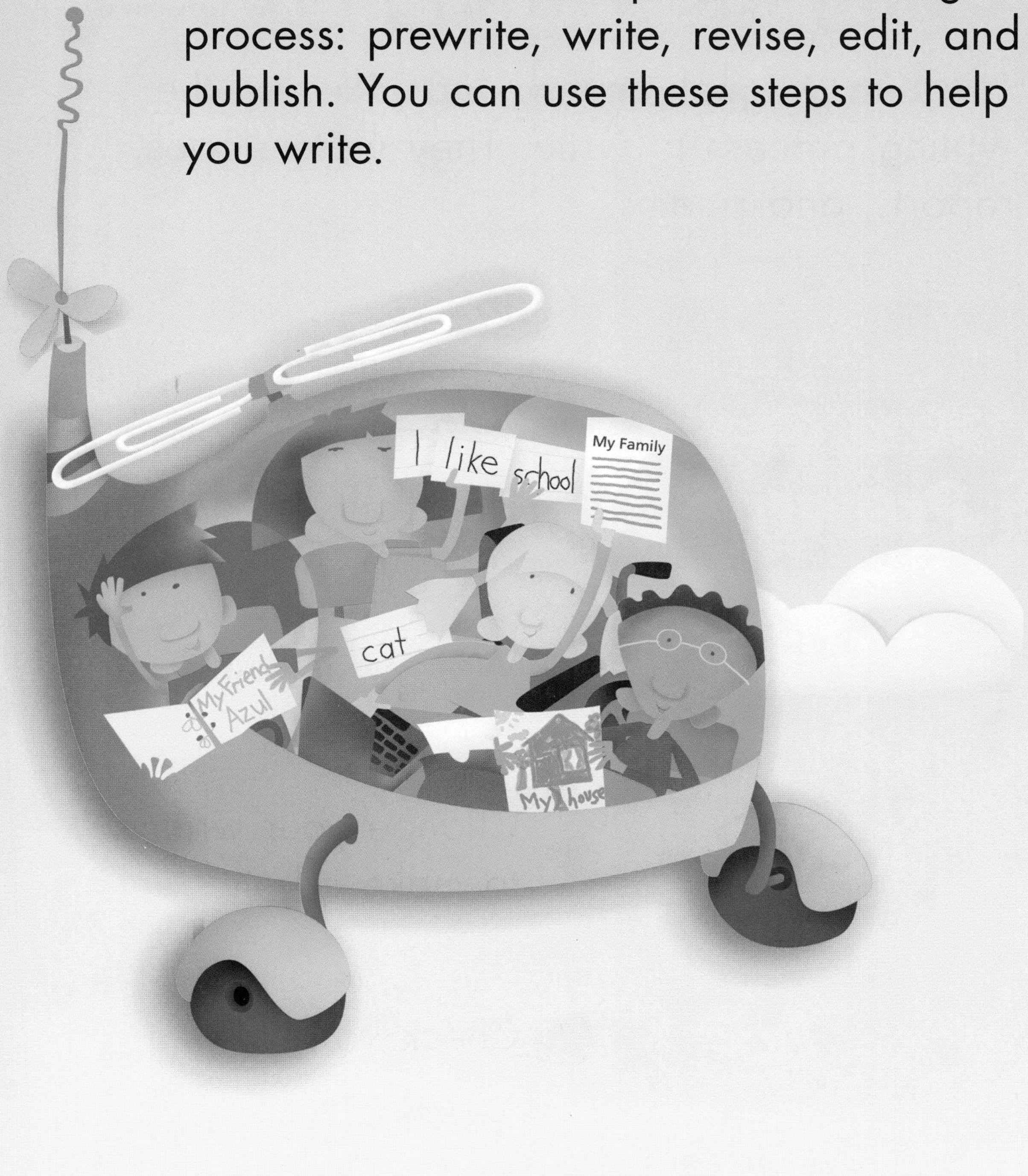

Using the Writing Process

Kim, Miguel, Emma, and Jake use the writing process to write. They write stories, reports, and poems.

The Writing Process

Prewrite ▶ Plan your writing.

Write ▶ Write your first draft.

Revise ▶ Change your writing to make it better.

Edit ▶ Check your writing.

Publish ▶ Share your writing.

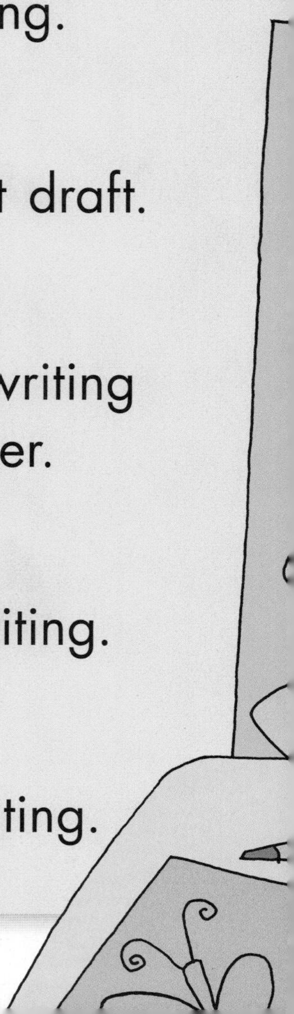

The Writing Process 15

One Writer's Process

Follow along and see how Kim uses the writing process to write a story about a living thing.

Prewrite

Prewriting is the first step in the writing process. When you **prewrite**, you plan your writing.

Here is what Kim does to plan her writing.

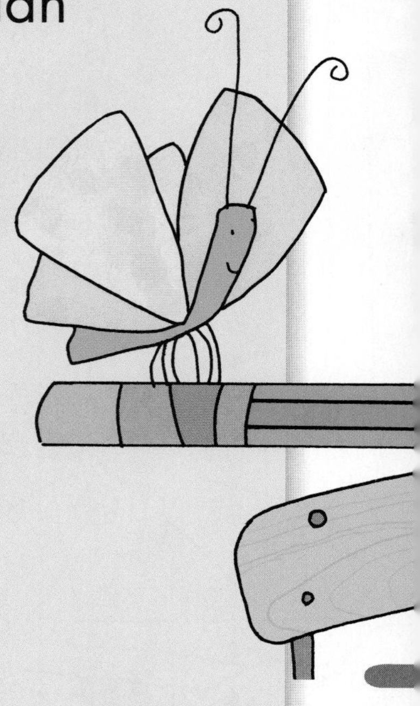

Think Kim thinks about living things.

List She lists her ideas.

Choose Kim chooses one idea as her topic.

Draw She draws a picture about her topic.

Kim's Prewriting

butterfly

rabbits

cat

Talk about it.

Tell what Kim does to plan her writing.

Write

When you **write a first draft**, you tell about your topic in sentences.

Here is what Kim does to write her first draft.

Look Kim looks at her picture to get ideas.

Think She thinks about what happened.

Write Then Kim writes her first draft.

Kim's First Draft

I saw a butterfly. the butterfly landed on my nose It tikld me.

Talk about it.

Tell what Kim does to write her first draft.

Revise

When you **revise**, you change your writing to make it better. Sometimes you add words to your writing.

Here is what Kim does to revise her writing.

Read Kim reads her first draft to a partner.

Listen She listens to her partner's questions.

Change Then Kim changes her writing.

Kim's Revising

I saw a ^yellow butterfly.

the butterfly landed

on my nose It tikld me.

Talk about it.

Tell what Kim does to revise her writing.

Edit

When you **edit** your writing, you check for capital letters, end marks, and spelling.

Here is what Kim does to edit her writing.

Read Kim reads her revised writing.

Check She checks her sentences for capital letters, end marks, and spelling.

Correct Kim corrects her sentences.

Kim's Editing

yellow T

I saw a ^ butterfly. the

butterfly landed on my

tickled

nose. It tikld me.

Talk about it.

Tell what Kim does to edit her writing.

Publish

When you **publish** your writing, you share it with others.

Here is what Kim does to publish her writing.

Think Kim thinks of a title for her story.

Write She writes a neat final copy of her story and finishes her picture.

Share Kim shares her writing with her friends.

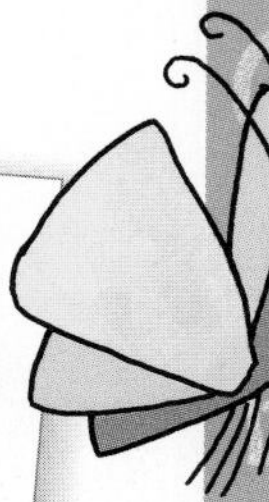

Kim's Published Story

My Butterfly

I saw a yellow butterfly. The butterfly landed on my nose. It tickled me.

Talk about it.

How does Kim publish her writing?

Working with a Partner

Working together can be fun. That's true for writers, too.

Here are some ways a partner can help you make your writing better.

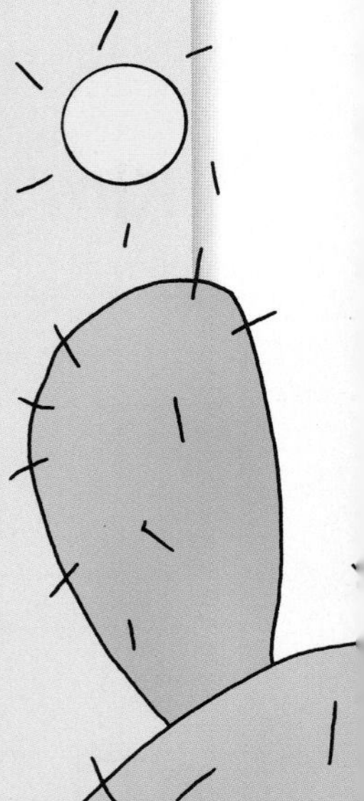

Listen A partner listens as you read your writing.

Ask A partner asks questions about your writing.

Talk A partner talks to you about your writing.

Cactus pears are yellow, orange, green, or red. They grow on a prickly pear cactus. Some people make salsa with cactus pears.

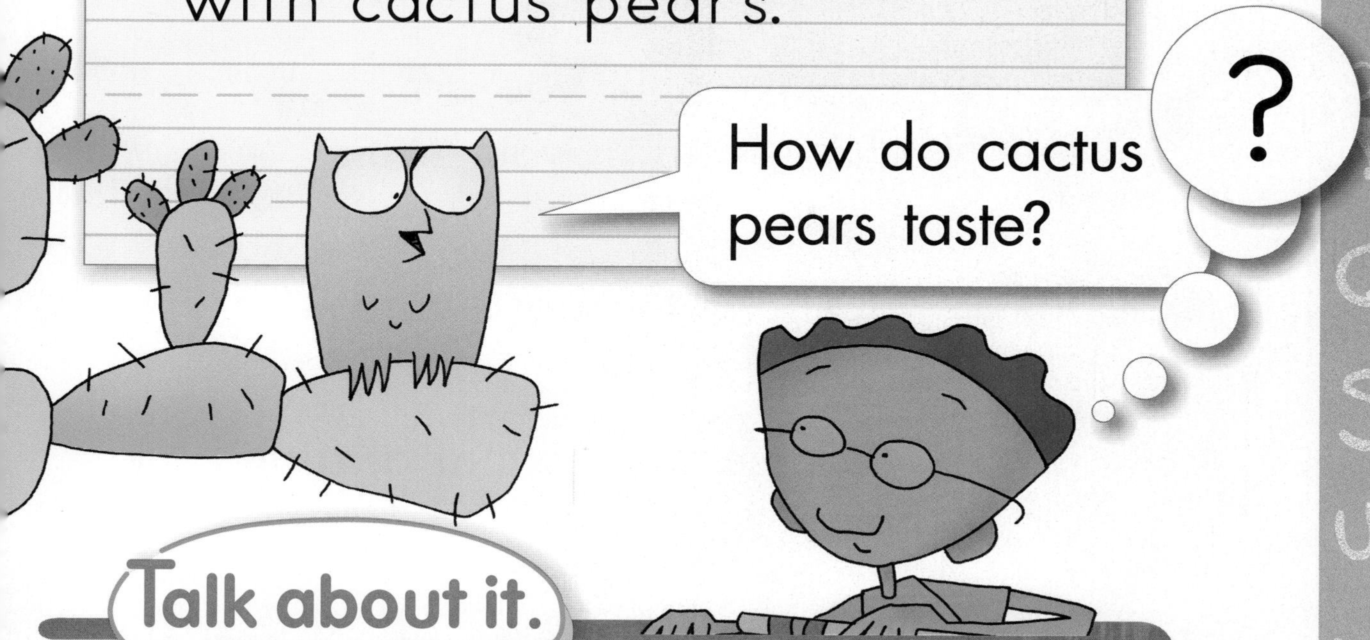

Talk about it.

How can partners help each other make their writing better?

Understanding the Writing Traits

You can use the *six traits* of writing listed below to become a better writer.

Start with great ideas.

Make your words and sentences easy to follow.

Sound as if you are really interested in your topic.

Choose the best words.

Use sentences that are fun to read.

Follow the rules for writing.

Use the traits.

Jake knows about the zoo. He writes about something that he saw.

Talk about it.

Tell a partner about something you have seen.

Ideas Start with great ideas.

Jake thinks about his trip to the zoo. He writes words about what he saw.

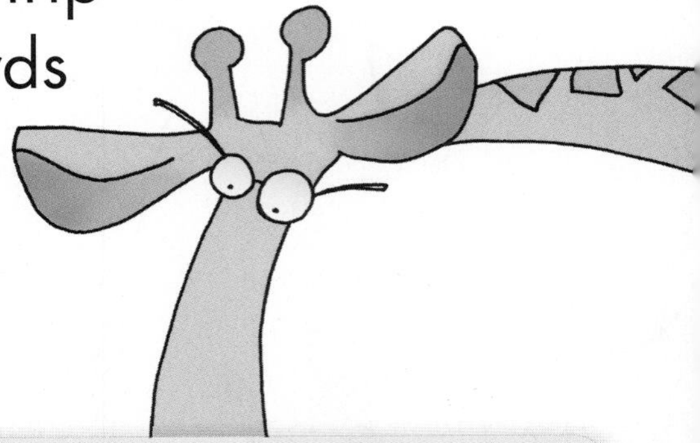

Talk about it.

Which words tell you what Jake saw?

Organization

Make your words and sentences easy to follow.

Jake organizes his ideas into sentences. He puts the words in an order that makes sense.

Organization

Talk about it.

Why did Jake put his words in order?

Voice

Sound as if you are really interested in your topic.

Jake adds words that sound as if he really likes his topic.

Voice

I saw a giraffe eating

and eating

Talk about it.

What words did Jake add to show his writing voice?

Word Choice

Choose the best words. They make a clear picture in the reader's mind.

Jake chooses a color word that makes a clear picture in the reader's mind.

Word Choice

I saw a giraffe eating

and eating green leaves

Talk about it.

What words did Jake add to make a clearer picture?

Sentence Fluency

Use sentences that are fun to read. You might use long and short sentences.

Jake adds another idea, but his writing is hard to read. He makes one long sentence and one short one. Now his writing is fun to read.

Sentence Fluency

I saw a giraffe eating and eating green leaves.

The giraffe was very hungry.

Talk about it.

How many sentences did Jake make?

Conventions **Follow the rules for writing.**

Jake follows the writing rules and makes a neat copy of his sentences. He uses capital letters and periods.

Talk about it.

How did Jake follow the writing rules?

Learning About a Rubric

A rubric lists the main traits for a form of writing. Jake and his teacher talk about the rubric below. It lists three traits. Now Jake knows what to look for in his writing.

Three Writing Traits	Great!
Ideas	Your writing has one topic and great details.
Organization	Your writing is in an order that makes sense.
Conventions	Your writing follows the writing rules.

Good	Keep Trying
Your writing has one topic and some details.	Your writing needs one topic and details.
Your writing shows some words and sentences in order.	Your writing needs order.
Your writing follows most of the writing rules.	Your writing needs to follow the rules.

Publishing Your Writing

When you **publish** your writing, you share it with others. Your teacher, friends, and family will enjoy reading about your ideas.

Here are some ways you can share your writing.

Make You can make a book.

Enter You can enter your writing on the computer and print a copy or send it by e-mail.

Post You can post your writing on a wall, door, or bulletin board.

Try other ways to publish.

Talk about it.

What ways have you used to publish your writing?

Using a Portfolio

A **portfolio** is a special place to save your writing. You add writing to your portfolio during the year. You can see how your writing is getting better and better.

Keep Use a folder or a box to keep your writing in one place.

Add During the year, add writing to your portfolio.

Look Take time to look at the writing in your portfolio. You can see how your writing is getting better.

Talk about it.

How do you save your writing?

WRITE SOURCE Online
www.hmheducation.com/writesource

Sentences and Paragraphs

Academic Vocabulary

Work with a partner. Read the meanings and share answers to the questions.

1. If something is **complete** it has no parts missing.
   If a meal is not complete, what might be missing?
2. **Order** means the way things follow one another.
   In what order do you brush your teeth?
3. **Related** words are words that go together in some way.
   Which word is related to the word *shirt*: *mouse* or *button*?

You think and talk about ideas. You can also write about your ideas in sentences. Then you can put the sentences together to make a paragraph.

Writing a Sentence

A **sentence** is a group of related words. It states a complete thought.

Kim thinks of words to write a sentence about a fox. You can use your own words to write sentences, too.

A sentence uses words to state a **complete thought**.

A sentence uses words in the **correct order**.

A sentence uses words that **name** and **tell**.

I saw a red fox today.

Talk about it.

Use your own words to finish each sentence.

1. The ant ________________.
2. ________________ digs holes.

Put your words in order.

The words in a sentence must be in the **correct order** to make sense.

These words are not in the correct order. They do not make sense.

fox A lives

woods the in

These words are in the correct order. They make sense.

A fox lives in the woods.

Talk about it.

Read each group of words. Tell which one makes sense.

1. Eyes has green cat the.
2. The cat has green eyes.

Find the naming part.

Every sentence has a naming part. The **naming part** tells who or what the sentence is about.

Naming Part

A fox lives in the woods.

Talk about it.

What is the **naming part** of each sentence?

1. My cat climbs the tree.
2. I jump up and down.
3. Mom looks up in the tree.
4. Dad gets a ladder.

Find the telling part.

Every sentence has a telling part. The **telling part** says something about the **naming part**.

Telling Part

A fox **lives in the woods.**

Talk about it.

What is the **telling part** of each sentence?

1. I throw a ball to Sadie.
2. She is our new puppy.
3. We play together.

Write complete sentences.

Remember that every sentence has a **naming part** and a **telling part**. See how these two parts go together.

Naming Part + **Telling Part**

The naming part tells who or what.

The telling part says something about the naming part.

=

Sentence

The naming part and telling part make a sentence. The sentence states a **complete thought**.

The fox hides.

Begin each sentence with a capital letter. Finish each sentence with an end mark.

Kinds of Sentences

Here are different kinds of sentences.

Telling Sentence

A **telling sentence** tells about something or someone.

A bird sits in the tree.

Asking Sentence

An **asking sentence** asks a question.

Do you see the bird?

Exclamatory Sentence

An **exclamatory sentence** shows surprise or strong feeling.

It has a huge bill!

Use end marks.

Every sentence needs an **end mark.**

Period.

Use a **period** at the end of a telling sentence.

Question Mark?

Use a **question mark** at the end of an asking sentence.

Exclamation Point!

Use an **exclamation point** at the end of an exclamatory sentence.

Talk about it.

Which **end mark** should you use?

1. I see a tiny bird ___
2. It is flying backward ___
3. Do you know its name ___

Writing a Paragraph

A **paragraph** is a group of sentences about the same topic.

Miguel uses sentences to write a paragraph. Here are some important points to remember when you write a paragraph.

A paragraph has a **beginning sentence** that tells the main idea.

A paragraph has **middle sentences** that tell more about the main idea. These sentences share details.

A paragraph has an **ending sentence** that adds one last thought.

A paragraph begins in a special way. You **indent**, or leave space, at the beginning of the paragraph.

The Park

Indent

One day, Mom took Elsa and me to the park. We climbed the jungle gym. Then we slid down the biggest slide. Finally, we played tag with friends. Wow! We had lots of fun at the park.

Miguel writes a paragraph.

Miguel uses the writing process to write his paragraph. This is how you can write a paragraph, too.

Prewrite

Choose a topic and gather details.

Write

Write your first draft.

E
One day, Mom took elsa
and me to the park. We climbed
Then
the jungle gym. we slid down the
Finally,
biggest slide. we played tag
friends Wow!
with freinds. We had lots of
fun at the park!

Revise

Change your writing to make it better.

Edit

Check your writing.

Publish

Make a final copy.

The Park

One day, Mom took Elsa and me to the park. We climbed the jungle gym. Then we slid down the biggest slide. Finally, we played tag with friends. Wow! We had lots of fun at the park!

WRITE SOURCE Online
www.hmheducation.com/writesource

Descriptive Writing

Academic Vocabulary

Work with a partner. Read the meanings and share answers to the questions.

1. Your **senses** are what you hear, smell, see, taste, and touch.
   Which one of your senses do you use the most?
2. When you **describe** something, you say what it is like.
   How would you describe your classroom?
3. **Details** are small facts.
   Name one detail about your house.

In **descriptive writing**, you use the five senses to create a picture in the reader's mind. You tell what something looks like, sounds like, smells like, feels like, or tastes like.

Literature Connections: You can find an example of descriptive writing in the article "Beaks Eat."

Descriptive Start-Up

In **descriptive writing**, you write sentences about what you see, hear, smell, taste, and touch.

Jake describes a tire swing.

Jake uses his senses to think of words that tell how the swing looks, sounds, and feels.

Remember these three points when you write a description.

1. You think about your topic.
2. You use your senses to get ideas.

3. You write describing words.

shiny black

squeaks smooth

Talk about it.

1. Choose something in your classroom.
2. Use your senses to think of describing words.
3. Describe the thing to a partner.

Descriptive Paragraph

Jake wrote some sentences to describe the tire swing at his school. Then he put his sentences together to form a paragraph.

Our Tire Swing

Our tire swing hangs from a wooden beam. A shiny chain holds the big black tire. The tire feels warm and smooth. The swing squeaks and creaks.

Understand your writing goal.

The three traits listed below will help you write a descriptive paragraph.

Ideas — Choose **one thing** to describe in your writing.

Word Choice — Use **describing words**.

Conventions — Follow the **writing rules**.

Talk about it.

1. What one thing does Jake describe?
2. Find describing words that Jake uses.
3. What is one writing rule that Jake follows?

Prewrite ▸ Choose your topic.

When you **prewrite**, you think about ideas and choose a topic.

Here is what Emma does to plan her writing.

Think Emma thinks of things she could describe.

List She lists ideas.

Choose She chooses one idea for her topic.

If you have a writing notebook, you can look for ideas there.

Emma's Topic List

Ideas

hamster

train

mouse

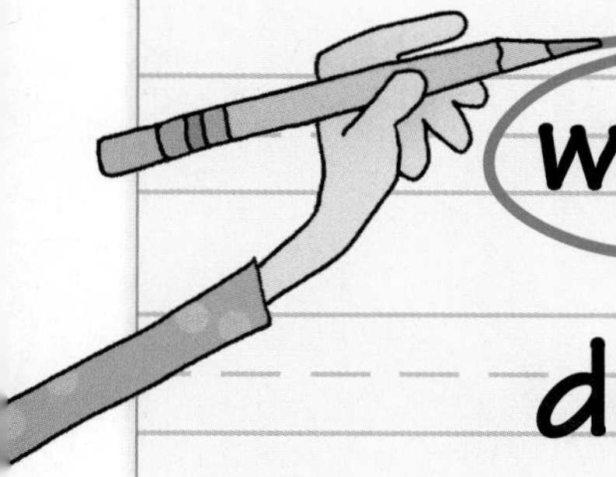

waffles

doll

Prewrite

Choose your topic.

1. **Think** of things you could describe.
2. **List** your ideas.
3. **Choose** your topic and circle it.

Prewrite ▸ Gather your details.

When you prewrite, you can use a sensory chart to gather details.

Here is what Emma does to gather her details.

Think Emma thinks of the last time she ate waffles.

Write She writes describing words about her topic on a sensory chart.

Emma's Sensory Chart

I will describe waffles. (topic)

see	brown square holes strawbarrys on top
hear	crunchy
smell	toasty
taste	yummy delicious juicy
touch	warm

Prewrite

Gather your details.

1. **Think** about your topic.
2. **Write** describing words about your topic on a sensory chart.

Write ▸ Write your first draft.

When you write a first draft, you put your ideas into sentences. Your **first draft** is your first try at writing about your topic.

Here is what Emma does to write her first draft.

Begin Emma begins with a sentence that introduces her topic.

Choose She chooses words from her sensory chart.

Write She uses those words to write sentences about her topic.

Emma's First Draft

Waffles are for breakfast.
They are brown with square holes.
strawbarrys sit on top.
They make a crunchy sound
Waffles are delicious!

Write

Write your first draft.

1. **Begin** with a sentence that introduces your topic.
2. **Choose** words from your sensory chart.
3. **Write** more sentences about your topic.

Revise ▸ Change your writing.

When you **revise**, you make changes in your writing. You try to make a clearer picture for the reader.

Here is what Emma does to make her writing better.

Read Emma reads her first draft to her partner.

Talk They talk about the use of sensory details. Her partner asks questions.

Change Emma makes changes. She adds more details to make a clearer picture.

A **caret** (^) shows where you add details to your writing.

Emma's Revising

Word Choice

Waffles are ^yummy for breakfast.
They are brown with square holes.
^Juicy strawbarrys sit on top.
^Waffles smell toasty. They make a crunchy sound
Waffles are delicious!

Revise

Change your writing to make it better.

1. **Read** your first draft to a partner.
2. **Talk** about sensory details.
3. **Change** your writing to make a clearer picture.

Edit ▸ Check your writing.

When you **edit**, you check your writing for conventions. You check for capital letters, end marks, and spelling.

Here's what Emma does to check her writing.

Read Emma reads her sentences.

Check She checks for capital letters, end marks, and spelling.

Mark She marks the changes she needs to make.

Emma's Editing

Conventions

Waffles are ^yummy for breakfast.

They are brown with square holes.

^Juicy ~~strawbarrys~~ strawberries sit on top.

^Waffles smell toasty. They make a crunchy sound.

Waffles are delicious!

Edit

Check your writing.

Use this checklist to edit your descriptive paragraph.

- ☑ Capital letters ≡
- ☑ End marks ⊙
- ☑ Spelling ◯

Publish ▸ **Make your final copy.**

When you **publish**, you make a neat final copy of your writing.

Here is what Emma does to publish her writing.

Skip Emma skips the first line to leave room for a title.

Indent She indents her first sentence. That means she leaves space at the beginning of her paragraph.

Copy Emma copies the rest of her corrected sentences in order.

Emma's Final Copy

Indent

Waffles are yummy for breakfast. They are brown with square holes. Juicy strawberries sit on top. Waffles smell toasty. They make a crunchy sound. Waffles are delicious!

Publish

Make your final copy.

1. **Skip** the first writing line.
2. **Indent** your first sentence.
3. **Copy** all your corrected sentences in order.

Publish

When you publish your writing, you share it.

Add a title and a drawing.

Delicious!

Waffles are yummy for breakfast. They are brown with square holes. Juicy strawberries sit on top. Waffles smell toasty. They make a crunchy sound. Waffles are delicious!

Publish

Share your writing.

Read your description to someone.

Reflect on your writing.

Emma thinks about her writing. She tells how she feels about her descriptive paragraph.

Thinking About Your Writing

1. I picked this topic because

   I love waffles!

2. The best thing about my writing is

   I use words like toasty and yummy.

Reflect

Think about your writing. On your own paper, finish the two sentences above.

Across the Curriculum

You may be asked to do descriptive writing for different school subjects.

Math

In math, Chaya describes a triangle. Her words make a picture for the reader. She also adds a drawing with labels.

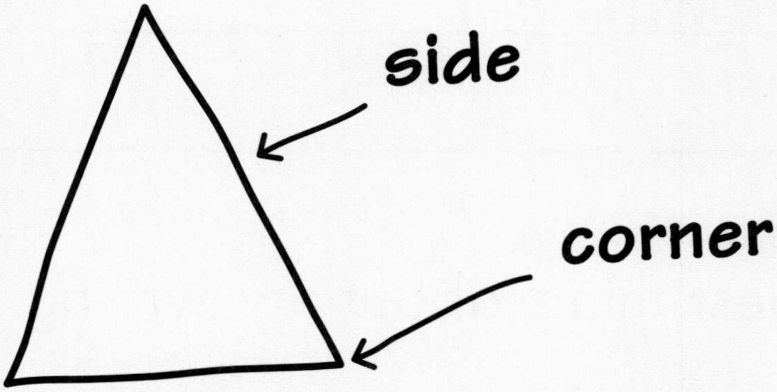

A Triangle

A triangle has three sides.
It has three corners.

Science

Carter uses his senses to describe the classroom pet in a paragraph.

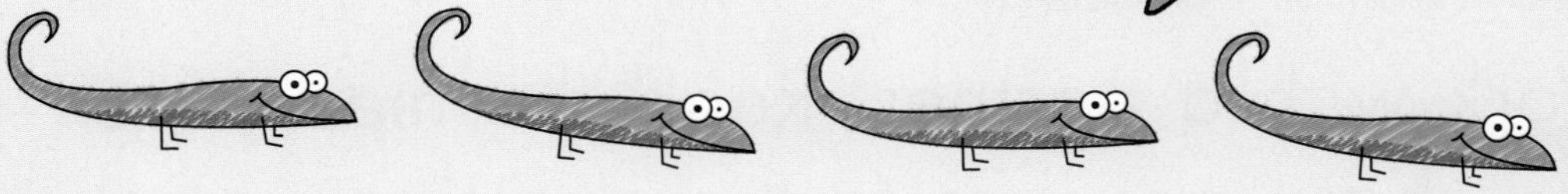

Lizzy, the Lizard

Our lizard has a long body and a long tail. Lizzy is an anole. She has four short legs and tiny toes. Lizzy is green and brown. Her skin feels smooth.

WRITE SOURCE Online
www.hmheducation.com/writesource

Narrative Writing

Academic Vocabulary

Work with a partner. Read the meanings and share answers to the questions.

1. If something is **special** it is the most important one.
   What is one special thing you like to do after school?
2. The **final** one is the last one.
   What is the final thing you do every day?

In **narrative writing**, you share a story about something that really happened. It can be about you or someone else. In this chapter, you will learn how to write about a special time.

Literature Connections: You can find an example of narrative writing in *Our Sled Club* by Beatrice Wolfe.

Narrative Start-Up

In a **personal narrative**, you write a story about something you did.

Kim writes about a special time.

Kim remembers a day with her grandma. She writes a first sentence about it.

Here are two points to remember when you write a personal narrative.

1. You remember one special time and what you did.

2. You use the word *I* to write about yourself.

One day, I had lunch with Grandma.

Talk about it.

Tell a partner about one special time that you remember.

Narrative Paragraph

Kim wrote more sentences about the special time with her grandma. Then she put her sentences together to form a paragraph.

Noodles

One day, I had lunch with Grandma. We made noodles. I put some noodles in the soup. Then I ate them. I like cooking with Grandma.

Understand your writing goal.

The three traits listed below will help you write a narrative paragraph.

Ideas — Choose **one special time** to write about.

Organization — Use **time-order words**.

Conventions — Follow the **writing rules**.

Talk about it.

1. What one special time does Kim share?
2. Find one writing rule that Kim follows.

Prewrite ▶ Choose your topic.

When you **prewrite**, you plan your writing. To get started, choose a topic.

Here is what Miguel does to choose his topic.

Think Miguel thinks about some special times.

Finish He finishes some sentence starters to get ideas.

Choose Miguel chooses his favorite idea as his topic.

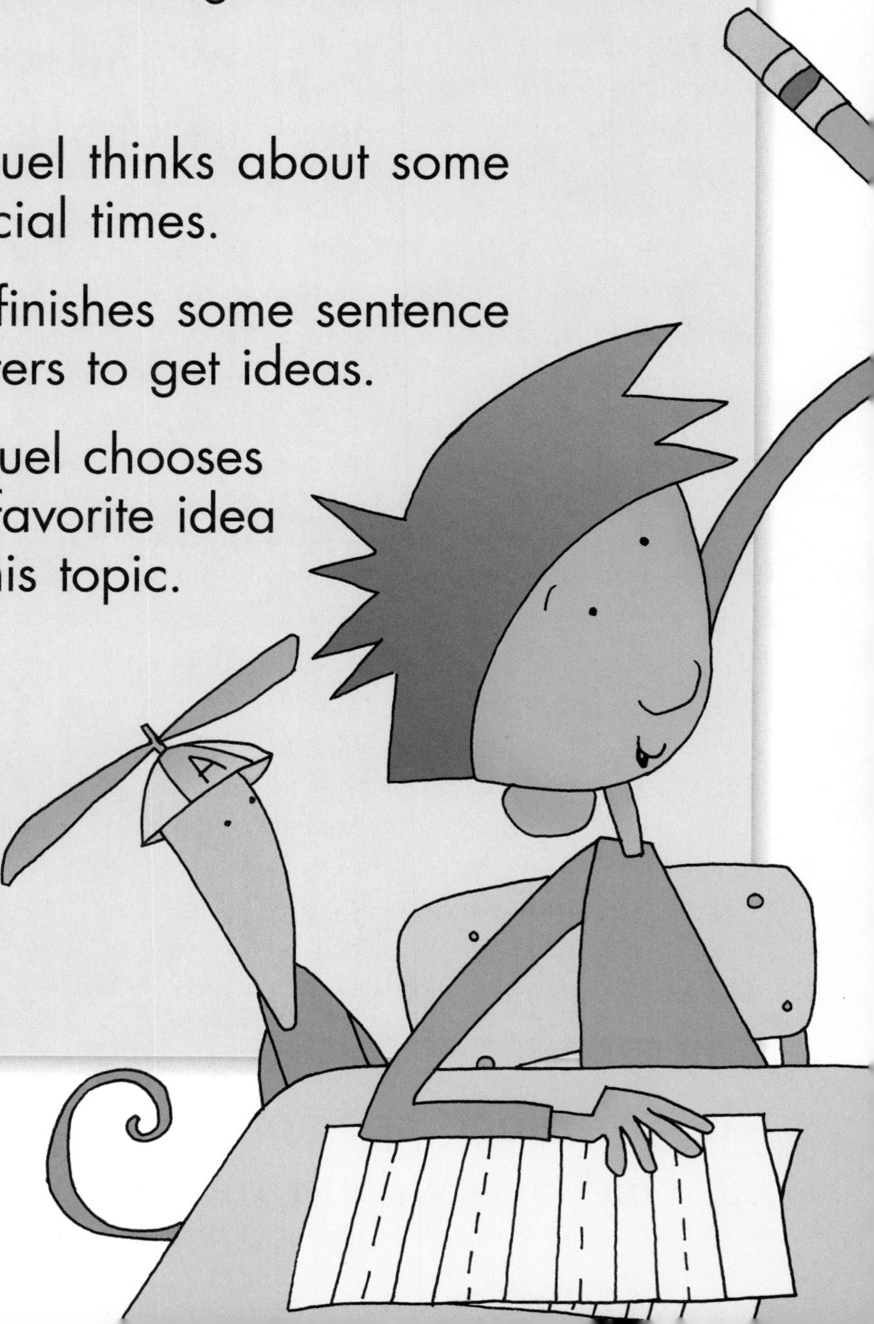

Miguel's Topic Ideas

Ideas

Sentence Starters

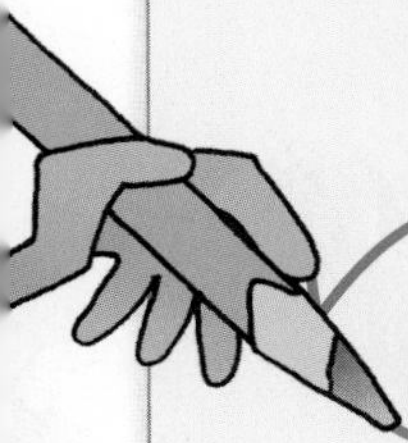

1. One summer, I went to Texas.
2. One day, I lost Azul at school.
3. One night, I saw an owl!

Prewrite

Choose your topic.

1. **Think** of some special times.
2. **Finish** each sentence starter with one idea.
3. **Choose** your topic and circle it.

Prewrite ▸ Gather your details.

Gathering details about your topic is the next part of prewriting. **Details** tell more about your topic.

Here is what Miguel does to gather his details.

Draw Miguel draws pictures on a story map.

Write He writes words that tell *who, what,* and *where.*

Tell Miguel tells his story to a partner.

Miguel's Story Map

Prewrite

Gather your details.

1. **Draw** a story map that shows what happened.
2. **Write** words that tell *who, what,* and *where.*
3. **Tell** your story to a partner using your story map.

Write ▸ Write your first draft.

When you write a first draft, you put your ideas into sentences. Your **first draft** is your first try at writing about your topic.

Here is what Miguel does to write his first draft.

Begin Miguel begins with his sentence starter.

Look Then he looks at his story map.

Write Miguel writes a sentence about each picture.

Sentence Starters

1. One summer, I went to Texas.

2. One day, I lost Azul at school.

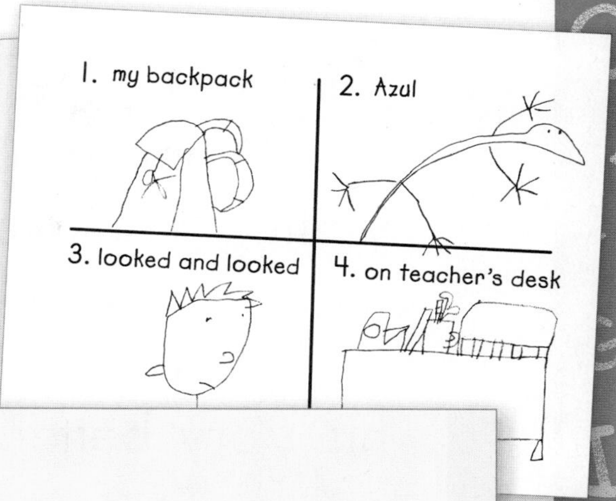

Miguel's First Draft

One day, I lost Azul at school.
I opened my backpack.
Azul jumt out.
I looked and looked
he was on my teacher's desk!

Write

Write your first draft.

1. **Begin** with your sentence starter.
2. **Look** at your story map.
3. **Write** a sentence for each picture.

Revise ▸ Change your writing.

When you **revise**, you change your writing to make it better.

Here is what Miguel does to make his story better.

Read Miguel reads his story to a partner.

Talk They talk about the story. Miguel's partner asks a question.

Change Miguel uses carets (∧) to show where he wants to add words. He answers his partner's question and adds a time-order word.

Time-order words tell when something happens.

Time-Order Words

then	soon
first	later
next	now

Miguel's Revising

Organization

Azul is my pet lizard.

One day, I lost Azul at school.^

I opened my backpack.

Then

^Azul jumt out.

I looked and looked

he was on my teacher's desk!

Revise

Change your writing to make it better.

1. **Read** your writing to a partner.
2. **Talk** about your story.
3. **Change** your writing to make it better.

Edit ▸ Check your writing.

When you **edit**, you check your writing for conventions. You check for capital letters, end marks, and spelling.

Here is what Miguel does to check his writing.

Read Miguel reads his sentences.

Check He checks for capital letters, end marks, and spelling.

Mark He marks the changes he needs to make.

Miguel's Editing

Conventions

Azul is my pet lizard.
One day, I lost Azul at school.^

I opened my backpack.

Then jumped
^Azul (jumt) out.

I looked and looked⊙
H
he was on my teacher's desk!
≡

Edit

Check your writing.

Use this checklist to edit your narrative paragraph.

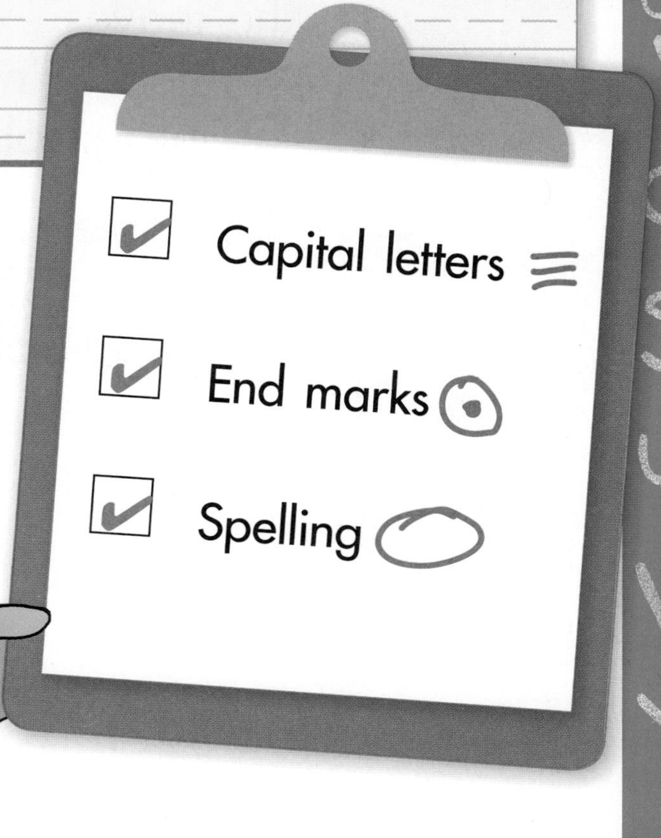

Publish ▸ Make your final copy.

When you **publish**, you make a neat final copy of your writing. You write your corrected sentences in paragraph form.

Here is what Miguel does to publish his paragraph.

Skip Miguel skips the first line to leave room for a title.

Indent Miguel indents his first sentence. That means he leaves extra space at the beginning of a paragraph.

Copy He copies the rest of his corrected sentences in paragraph form.

Azul is my pet lizard.
One day, I lost Azul at school. ^
I opened my backpack.
Then jumped
^ Azul (jumt) out.
I looked and looked ⊙
H
he was on my teacher's desk!

Indent

One day, I lost Azul at school. Azul is my pet lizard. I opened my backpack. Then Azul jumped out. I looked and looked. He was on my teacher's desk!

Publish

Make your final copy.

1. **Skip** your first writing line.
2. **Indent** your first sentence.
3. **Copy** your corrected sentences in paragraph form.

Publish ▸ Share your writing.

When you publish your writing, you share it with others.

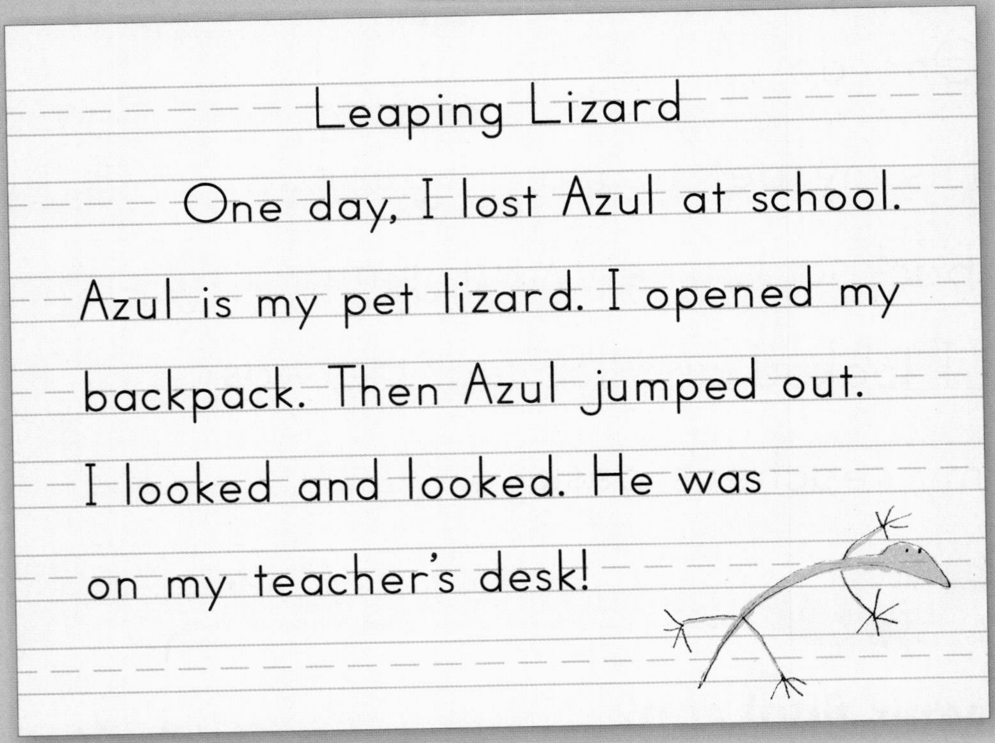

Leaping Lizard

One day, I lost Azul at school. Azul is my pet lizard. I opened my backpack. Then Azul jumped out. I looked and looked. He was on my teacher's desk!

Publish

Share your writing.

Read your narrative to someone.

Reflect on your writing.

Miguel thinks about his writing. He tells how he feels about his narrative paragraph.

Thinking About Your Writing

1. I picked this topic because

Azul always surprises me.

2. The best thing about my writing is

the happy ending.

Reflect

Think about your writing. On your own paper, finish the two sentences above.

Across the Curriculum

You may be asked to do narrative writing for some of your school subjects.

Reading

Nola writes a letter to an author, Mercer Mayer. She shares a story related to his book.

October 5, 2011

Dear Mr. Mayer,

I read the story <u>You're the Scaredy Cat</u>. Once I tried to camp in my yard. It rained. I had to go inside, too. I love your books! I want to read all of them.

Your fan,

Nola

Music

Len writes about one special time when music made him happy.

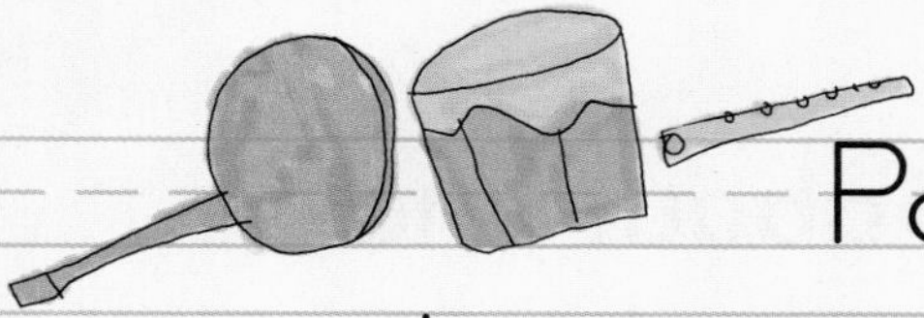

Powwow

Last summer, I went to a powwow. Many people came. Grandfather played the water drum. Dad played a wood flute. I got to shake a turtle shell rattle. Later we danced. The music made me happy. I like powwows.

Writing for Assessment

Wendy's teacher gives her a special writing idea called a **prompt**. Wendy reads the prompt, makes a story map, and writes her paragraph.

Writing Prompt

Write a story about one time when you had fun.

Wendy's Story Map

Wendy's Writing

Pumpkin Farm

I had fun at the pumpkin farm. First, I picked out a big pumpkin. It was heavy! Mom and I rode on a hay wagon. Then we went to a big red barn. We ate apples. I like the pumpkin farm.

WRITE SOURCE Online
www.hmheducation.com/writesource

Expository Writing

Academic Vocabulary

Work with a partner. Read the meanings and share answers to the questions.

1. To **share** something with others means to tell them your ideas or feelings.
   What would you like to share with a friend?
2. If you **gather** things you collect them together.
   What kinds of things can you gather in a park?

In **expository writing**, you share information about something or explain how to do something. In this chapter, you will practice explaining how to do something.

Literature Connections: You can find an example of expository writing in "Drums" by Tim Pano.

Expository Start-Up

In a **how-to paragraph**, you write sentences that explain how to do something.

Miguel explains an experiment.

Miguel likes science class. He writes about an experiment that he did.

Here are two points to remember when you write a how-to paragraph.

1. You think about something you know how to do well.
2. You list all the steps in order.

Miguel's Order Chart

Topic: How to Make a Penny Bright

Step 1	**old penny**	
Step 2	**lemon juice**	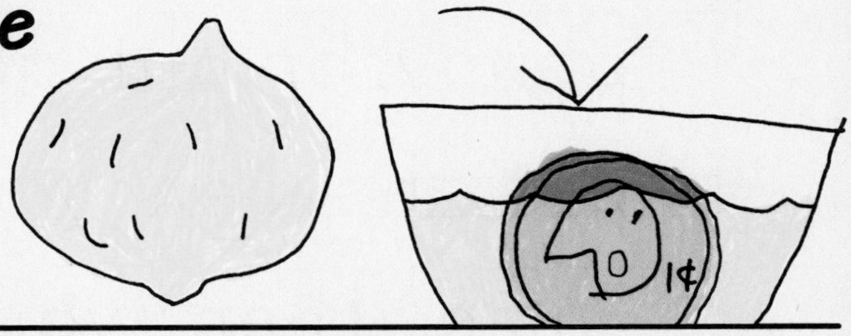
Step 3	**shiny penny**	

Talk about it.

With a partner, talk about things you know how to do.

Expository Paragraph

Miguel wrote sentences about his experiment. Then he put his sentences in order to form a paragraph.

Make a Penny Shine

You can make an old penny bright again. First, put the penny in lemon juice. Then wait five minutes. Finally, take out the shiny penny!

Understand your writing goal.

The three traits below will help you write a how-to paragraph.

Ideas	Think of **something you can explain.**
Organization	Put the **steps in order.**
Conventions	Follow the **writing rules.**

Talk about it.

1. What does Miguel explain?
2. Find time-order words that Miguel uses to put his steps in order.
3. Find one writing rule Miguel follows.

Prewrite ▸ Choose your topic.

When you **prewrite**, you plan your writing. Sometimes you list your ideas to find a writing topic.

Here is what Emma does to choose a topic.

Think Emma thinks of things that she could explain.

List She lists the activities that she thinks of.

Choose Emma chooses her topic.

Emma's Activity List

Ideas

plant a flower
make a sandwich
draw a cat
make green paint
braid yarn

Prewrite

Choose your topic.

1. **Think** of things you do well.
2. **List** activities on your own paper.
3. **Choose** your writing topic and circle it.

Prewrite ▸ Gather your details.

When you prewrite, you can use an order chart to gather details.

Here is what Emma does to gather her details.

Think Emma thinks of each step she follows to make green paint.

Draw She draws a picture to show each step on her order chart.

Label Emma labels all of her pictures.

Emma's Order Chart

Organization

Topic: How to Make Green Paint

Step 1	
Step 2	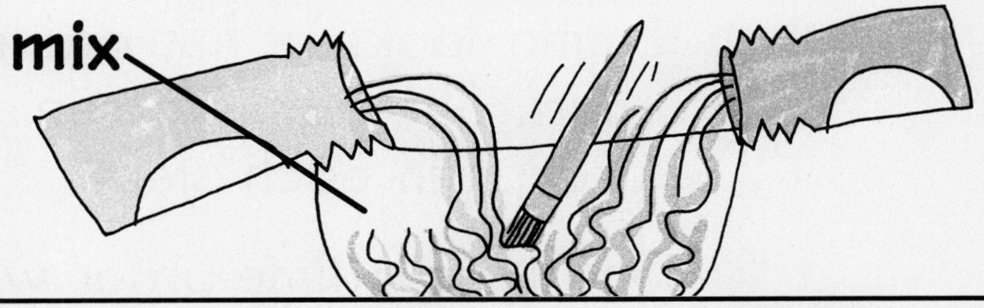
Step 3	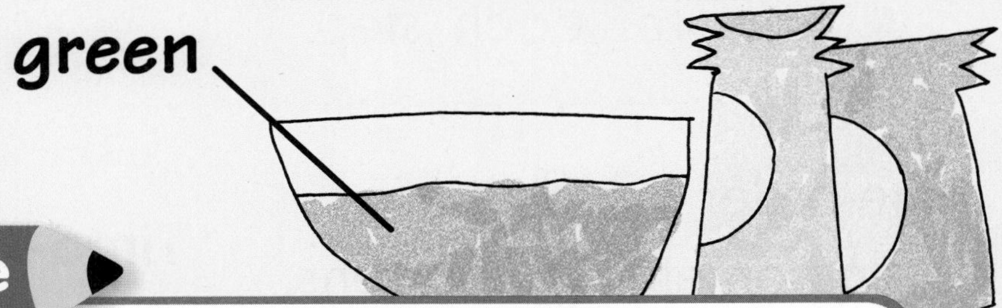

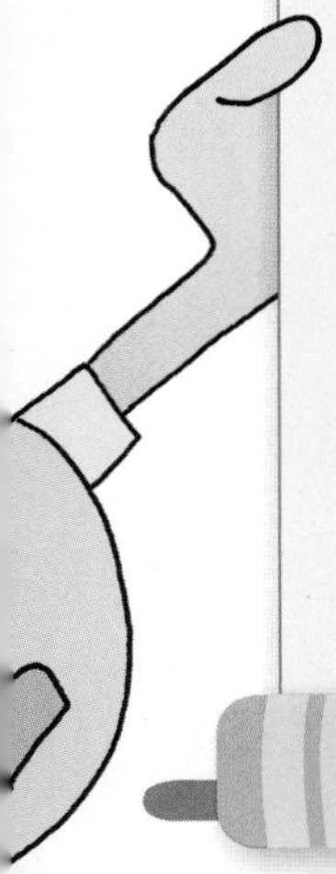

Prewrite

Gather your details.

1. **Think** of each of your how-to steps.
2. **Draw** a picture to show each step.
3. **Label** each of your pictures.

Write ▶ **Write your first draft.**

When you write a first draft, you put your ideas into sentences. Your **first draft** is your first try at writing about your topic.

Here is what Emma does to write her first draft.

Start Emma writes a first sentence that starts with **You can**.

Write Emma looks at her order chart. She writes a sentence to explain each step.

Use She uses a time-order word for each step.

Time-order words tell when something happens.

Time-Order Words

first	second
then	next
after	now

You can make green paint.
First, get yellow paint and blue paint
Then mix both of the paints togethr.
now, the two colors make green paint.

Write

Write your first draft.

1. **Start** with a **You can** sentence.
2. **Write** a sentence for each of your steps.
3. **Use** a time-order word for each step.

Revise ▸ Change your writing.

When you **revise**, you make changes in your writing to make it better.

Here is what Emma does to make her writing better.

Read Emma reads her first draft to a partner.

Listen Emma wants her how-to paragraph to be clear. She listens to her partner's ideas.

Change She uses carets (∧) to show where she wants to add to her writing. She adds a missing detail and a feeling word.

Emma's Revising

You can make green paint.

First, get yellow paint and blue paint

use a paintbrush to

Then ^ mix both of the paints togethr.

Wow!

now, the two colors make green paint. ^

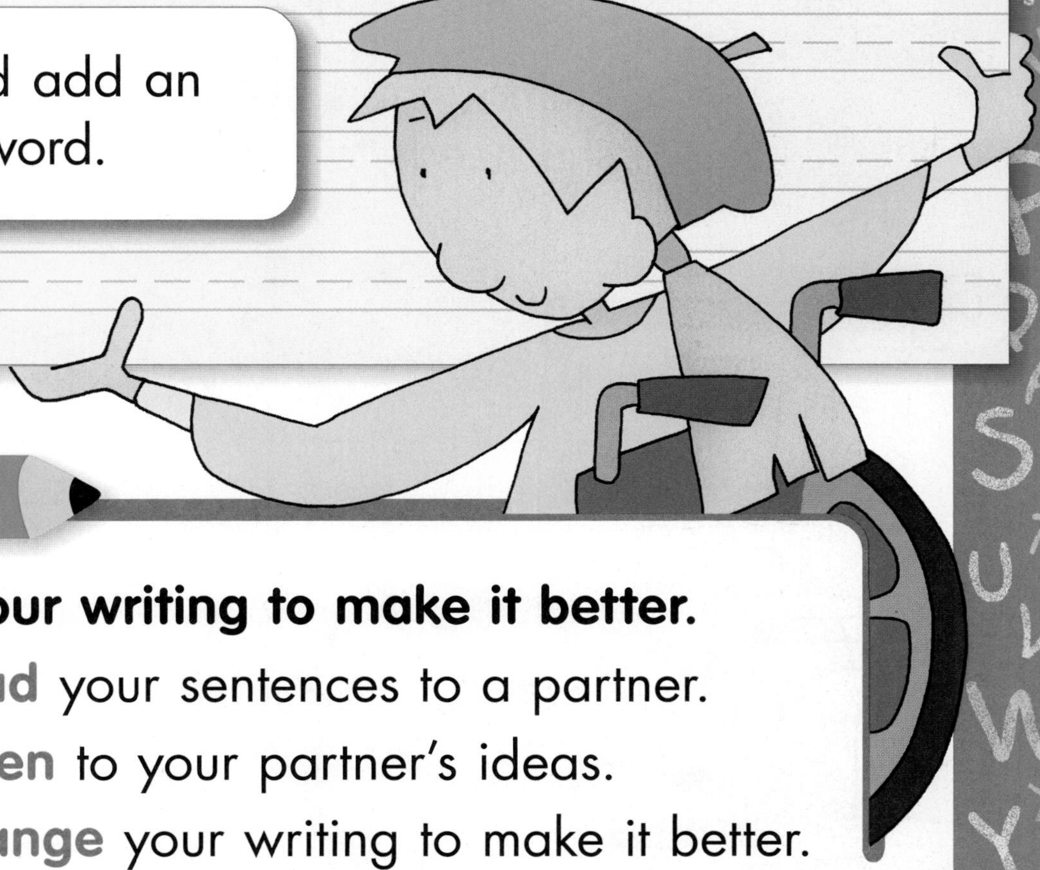

Revise

Change your writing to make it better.

1. **Read** your sentences to a partner.
2. **Listen** to your partner's ideas.
3. **Change** your writing to make it better.

Edit ▸ Check your writing.

When you **edit**, you check your writing for conventions. You check for capital letters, end marks, and spelling.

Here is what Emma does to check her writing.

Read Emma reads her sentences.

Check She checks for capital letters, end marks, and spelling.

Mark Emma marks the changes she needs to make.

Emma's Editing

Conventions

You can make green paint.

First, get yellow paint and blue paint.

use a paintbrush to ... together

Then ^ mix both of the paints togethr.

N ... Wow!

now, the two colors make green paint. ^

≡

Edit

Check your writing.

Use this checklist to edit your how-to paragraph.

- ☑ Capital letters ≡
- ☑ End marks ○
- ☑ Spelling ○

Publish ▸ Make your final copy.

When you **publish**, you make a neat final copy of your writing.

Here is what Emma does to publish her writing.

Skip Emma skips the first line to leave room for a title.

Indent She indents her first sentence. This means she leaves an extra space at the beginning of her first line.

Copy She copies the rest of her corrected sentences in paragraph form.

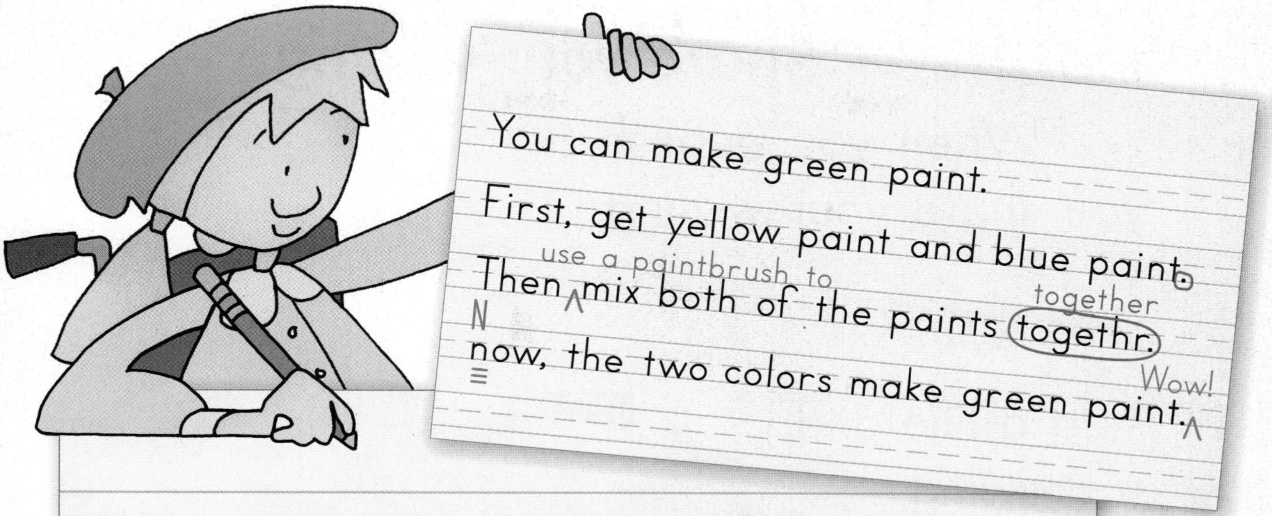

Indent

You can make green paint. First, get yellow paint and blue paint. Then use a paintbrush to mix both of the paints together. Now, the two colors make green paint. Wow!

Publish

Write your paragraph.

1. **Skip** the first writing line.
2. **Indent** your first sentence.
3. **Copy** your corrected sentences in paragraph form.

Publish ▸ Share your writing.

When you publish, you share your writing.

Make Green Paint

You can make green paint. First, get yellow paint and blue paint. Then use a paintbrush to mix both of the paints together. Now, the two colors make green paint. Wow!

Publish

Share your writing.

Read your how-to paragraph to someone.

Reflect on your writing.

Emma thinks about her writing. She tells how she feels about her how-to paragraph.

Thinking About Your Writing

1. I picked this topic because
   I like to paint pictures.

2. The best thing about my writing is
   my steps are in the correct order.

Reflect

Think about your writing. On your own paper, finish the two sentences above.

Across the Curriculum

You may be asked to do expository writing for different school subjects. You share information about what you learn.

Math

Tyler writes about a math problem. He draws a picture. It helps him explain addition.

2 + 3 = 5

Adding Numbers

You can add 2 + 3. First, draw dots. Make a set of two dots. Then make a set of three dots. Finally, count all of the dots. Make five dots. You can see that 2 + 3 = 5.

Social Studies

Maya learns about the Havasupai Indian tribe. They live in Arizona. She writes a paragraph about them.

Collar Makers

Indian tribes live in Arizona. One tribe lives at the bottom of the Grand Canyon. They are the people of the blue and green waters. They make collars with tiny beads. Can you guess what color beads they like to use?

Writing for Assessment

Alano's teacher gives him an expository **prompt** to write about. Alano reads the prompt, makes a cluster, and writes a paragraph.

Writing Prompt

In a paragraph, explain something new you have learned.

Alano's Cluster

Alano's Writing

Coins

Collecting coins is an interesting hobby. Coins can be silver, gold, or copper. They come from many countries. Some coins are very old. It is easier to find new coins.

Persuasive Writing

Academic Vocabulary

Work with a partner. Read the meanings and share answers to the questions.

1. A **reason** explains why something happened.
   What is a reason someone might be late for school?
2. If you **agree** with someone, you think the same thing about something.
   What kinds of things do you and a friend agree on?

In **persuasive writing,** you share your opinion. You give reasons why others should agree with you.

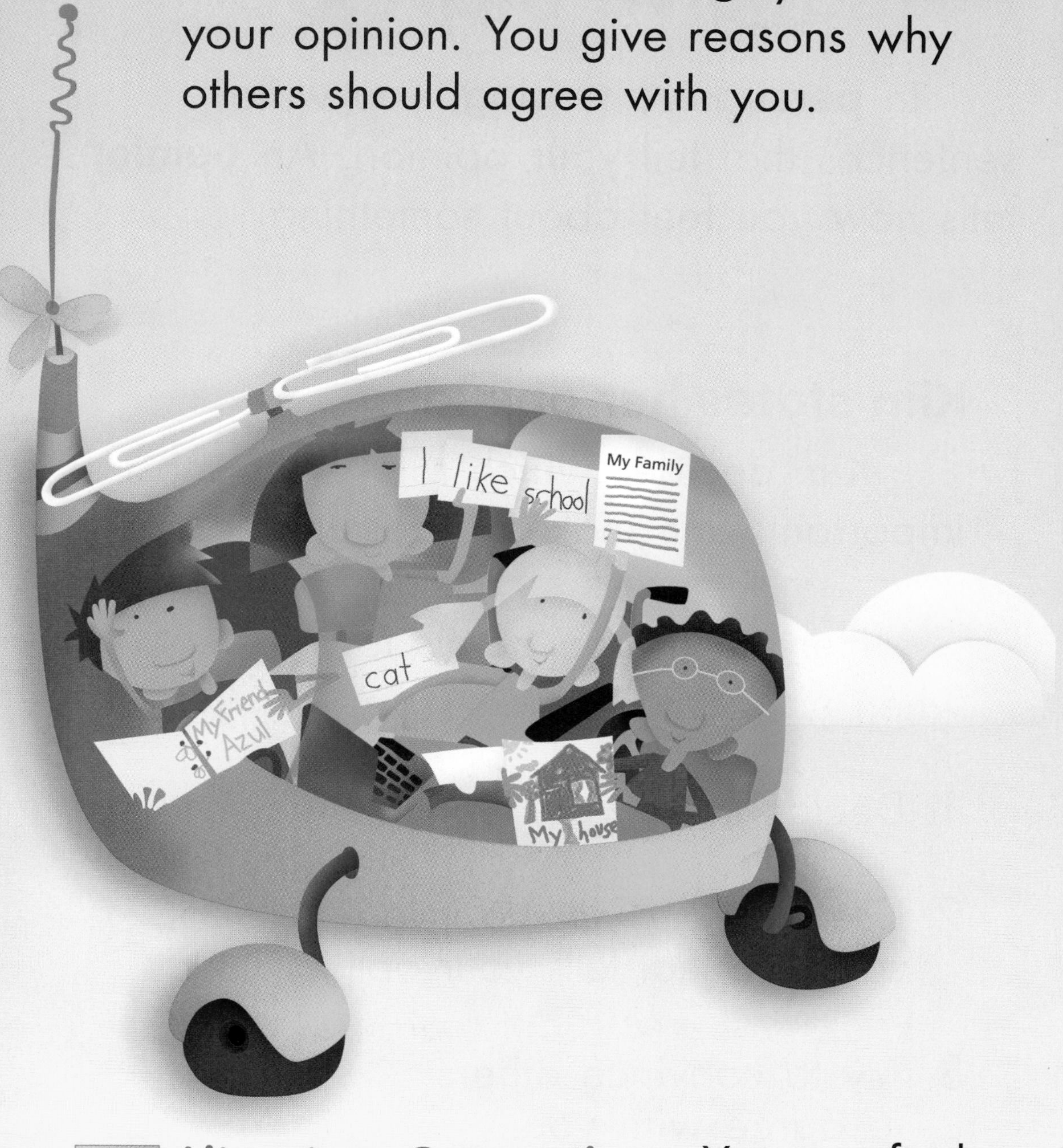

Literature Connections: You can find an example of persuasive ideas in the article "Three Reasons Why Pets are Great."

Persuasive Start-Up

In **persuasive writing,** you write sentences that tell your opinion. An **opinion** tells how you feel about something.

Kim states her opinion.

Kim decides which rule is the most important. She makes a poster about it.

Here are three points to remember when you write to persuade.

1. Decide what your opinion is.
2. Use the word *should* in a sentence that tells your opinion.
3. Try to convince others to agree with you.

Talk about it.

1. Talk about your school rules.
2. Decide which rule is most important.
3. Use the word *should* in a sentence that tells your opinion.

Persuasive Paragraph

Kim looks at her poster. She writes some sentences about why the rule is important. Then she puts them together in a paragraph.

Prewrite ▸ Gather your reasons.

When you **prewrite**, you make a list to gather reasons for your opinion.

Kim lists three reasons to follow the rule.

My Reasons

1. to be quiet
2. to see where we are going
3. to stay safe

Prewrite

Gather your reasons.

List reasons to follow the rule.

Write ▸ Write your first draft.

When you write a **first draft**, you put your reasons into sentences.

Kim starts with her opinion sentence. Then she writes a sentence for each reason. Her last sentence repeats the rule.

We should walk in the halls it helps us be quiet. We can see where we are going. Walking helps everyone stay safe. Always walk in the halls.

Write

Write your first draft.

1. **Start** with your opinion sentence.
2. **Write** a sentence for each reason.
3. **Repeat** the rule in a new way.

Revise ▸ Change your writing.

When you **revise**, you make changes in your writing. You add words that will get the reader to do something.

Kim reads her writing and talks about it with a partner. Then she adds another idea.

We should walk in the halls it helps us be quiet. We can see where we are going. Walking helps everyone stay safe. ^Be sure you^ Always walk in the halls.

Revise

Change your writing to make it better.

1. **Read** your writing.
2. **Talk** about your writing with a partner.
3. **Make** changes to help the reader.

Edit ▸ Check your writing.

When you **edit**, you check your writing for conventions. You check for capital letters, end marks, and spelling.

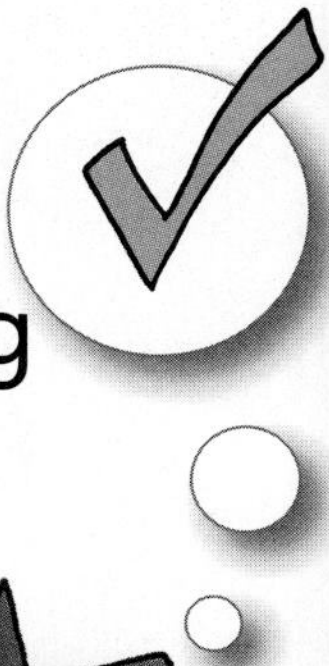

Kim uses a checklist. Then she marks changes.

I

We should walk in the halls. it helps us be quiet. We can see where we are going. Walking helps everyone

Be sure you a

stay safe. Always walk in the halls.

Edit

Check your writing.

Use this checklist to edit your persuasive paragraph.

- ☑ Capital letters ≡
- ☑ End marks ⊙
- ☑ Spelling ◯

Publish ▸ Share your writing.

When you **publish**, you make a neat final copy of your writing to share.

Kim adds a title. Then she copies the rest of her corrected sentences in paragraph form.

Please Walk

We should walk in the halls. It helps us be quiet. We can see where we are going. Walking helps everyone stay safe. Be sure you always walk in the halls.

Publish

Share your writing.

Make a neat copy. Read it to the class.

Across the Curriculum

Health

Pat writes a note to his mom. He shares his opinion about a healthy food choice.

WRITE SOURCE Online
www.hmheducation.com/writesource

Responding to Literature

Academic Vocabulary

Work with a partner. Read the meanings and share answers to the questions.

1. When you **respond** to someone, you say something back to them. **How would you respond if someone gave you a gift?**
2. A **fact** is something that is true. **Name one fact about your life.**
3. A **poem** is a piece of writing. Poems usually have short lines with words that rhyme at the end. **If you wrote a poem what would it be about?**

Responding to literature means talking and writing about what you read. You can respond to books that tell make-believe stories or facts. You can respond to poems, too.

Reviewing a Fiction Book

Books that tell make-believe stories are called **fiction** books.

Bay writes a book review.

Bay likes to read make-believe stories. He wrote a book review about *The Mysterious Tadpole* by Steven Kellogg.

Remember these points when you write a fiction book review.

The **Beginning** names the title and the author.

The **Middle** tells what the book is about and gives the main problem.

The **Ending** tells why you like the book.

Bay's Book Review

Growing Up

Beginning I read The Mysterious Tadpole by Steven Kellogg. Louis gets a tadpole from his uncle. The

Middle problem is that his tadpole grows and grows into something very unusual! I like this book because it

Ending made me laugh.

Prewrite ▸ Gather your details.

Before you can write a book review, you must choose a book and gather details about it.

List Emma lists titles and authors of books she likes.

Circle She circles the one she wants to write about.

Gather She gathers details on a details sheet.

Emma's Details Sheet

Details Sheet

1. I read Yoko
   by Rosemary Wells.
2. The story is about Yoko. She likes to eat sushi for lunch.
3. The problem is that the other animals think her sushi is strang.
4. I like this book because Yoko makes a new friend.

Prewrite

Choose your book and gather details.

1. **List** titles and authors of fiction books you like.
2. **Circle** the book you will review.
3. **Gather** details about your book on a details sheet.

Write ▸ Write your first draft.

When you write, you put your ideas into sentences.

Write Emma writes the sentences from her details sheet to tell about her book.

I read <u>Yoko</u> by Rosemary Wells. The story is about Yoko. She likes to eat sushi for lunch the problem is that the other animals think her sushi is strang. I like this book because Yoko makes a new friend.

Write

Write your first draft.

Write the sentences from your details sheet.

Revise ▸ Change your writing.

When you revise, you change your writing to make it better.

Read Emma reads her first draft to a partner.

Add Emma adds two new details.

I read Yoko by Rosemary Wells.
                       a cat named
The story is about ^Yoko. She likes to
eat sushi for lunch the problem is that
the other animals think her sushi is
                                     it has a happy ending.
strang. I like this book because ^Yoko
makes a new friend.

Revise

Change your writing to make it better.

1. **Read** your first draft to a partner.
2. **Add** more details to your writing.

Edit ▸ Check your writing.

When you edit, you check your writing for conventions. You check for capital letters, end marks, and spelling.

Here is what Emma does to edit her writing.

I read Yoko by Rosemary Wells. The story is about [a cat named] Yoko. She likes to eat sushi for lunch. [T]the problem is that the other animals think her sushi is strang [strange]. I like this book because [it has a happy ending.] Yoko makes a new friend.

Edit

Check your writing.

Use this checklist to edit your book review.

- [x] Capital letters ≡
- [x] End marks ⊙
- [x] Spelling ◯

Publish ▶ Share your writing.

When you publish, you make a neat final copy of your review to share.

Sushi Cat

I read Yoko by Rosemary Wells. The story is about a cat named Yoko. She likes to eat sushi for lunch. The problem is that the other animals think her sushi is strange. I like this book because it has a happy ending. Yoko makes a new friend.

Publish

Share your writing.

1. **Make** a neat final copy.
2. **Read** it to the class.

Reviewing a Nonfiction Book

Books about real facts are called **nonfiction**.

Linda writes a book review.

In her review, Linda shares the most interesting facts from *I Want to Be an Astronaut* by Byron Barton.

Remember these points when you write a nonfiction book review.

The **Beginning** names the title and the author.

The **Middle** tells what the book is about and shares interesting facts.

The **Ending** tells why you like the book.

Linda's Book Review

Riding in Space

Beginning

I read I Want to Be an Astronaut by Byron Barton. This book is about riding in a space shuttle.

Middle

I learned that astronauts sleep in zero gravity. They use seat belts to hold them in bed! Then they won't float around.

Ending

I like this book because someday I want to fly in space.

Prewrite ▸ Gather your facts.

Before you can write a book review, you must choose a book and gather interesting facts from it.

Choose Miguel chooses a book about science. He wants to be a scientist someday.

Read Miguel reads his book.

Gather He gathers facts on a fact sheet.

Miguel's Fact Sheet

Fact Sheet

1. I read What Is a Scientist?
by Barbara Lehn.

2. The book is about what scientists do.

3. I learned that scientists ask a lot of questions. They do exparaments. Sometimes they keep trying again and again.

4. I like this book because science is my best subject.

Prewrite

Choose your book and gather facts.

1. **Choose** a nonfiction book to review.
2. **Read** your book.
3. **Gather** facts from your book on a fact sheet.

Write ▸ Write your first draft.

When you write, you put your ideas into sentences.

Write Miguel writes the sentences from his fact sheet to tell about his book.

I read What Is a Scientist? by Barbara Lehn. The book is about what scientists do. I learned that scientists ask a lot of questions. They also do exparaments. Sometimes they keep trying again and again I like this book because science is my best subject.

Write

Write your first draft.

Write the sentences from your fact sheet.

Revise ▶ Change your writing.

When you revise, you change your writing to make it better.

Read Miguel reads his first draft to a partner.

Add He adds a detail.

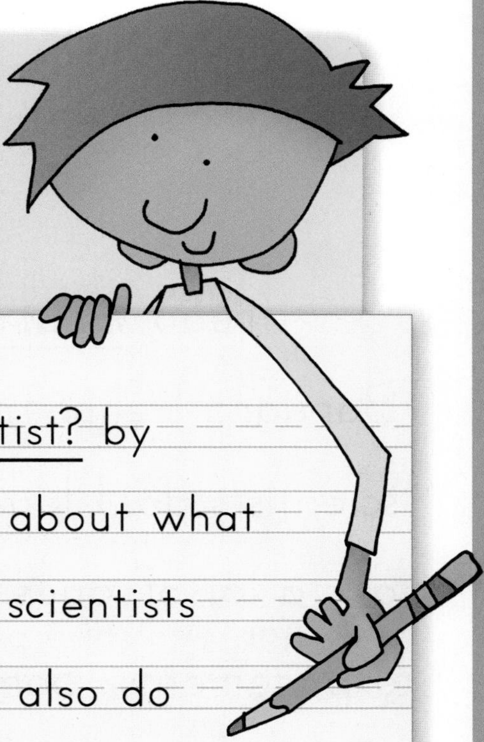

I read <u>What Is a Scientist?</u> by Barbara Lehn. The book is about what scientists do. I learned that scientists ask a lot of questions. They also do
to solve problems
exparaments^. Sometimes they keep trying again and again I like this book because science is my best subject.

Revise

Change your writing to make it better.

1. **Read** your first draft to a partner.
2. **Add** a detail or two to your writing.

Edit ▸ Check your writing.

When you edit, you check your writing for conventions.

Check Miguel checks his review.

I read <u>What Is a Scientist?</u> by Barbara Lehn. The book is about what scientists do. I learned that scientists ask a lot of questions. They also do ~~exparaments~~ experiments to solve problems. Sometimes they keep trying again and again. I like this book because science is my best subject.

Edit

Check your writing.

Use this checklist to edit your book review.

- ☑ Capital letters ≡
- ☑ End marks ⊙
- ☑ Spelling ◯

Publish ▸ Share your writing.

When you publish your review, you make a neat final copy.

Scientists

I read What Is a Scientist? by Barbara Lehn. The book is about what scientists do. I learned that scientists ask a lot of questions. They do experiments to solve problems. Sometimes they keep trying again and again. I like this book because science is my best subject.

Publish

Share your writing.

Read your book review to the class.

Writing for Assessment

Shane's teacher gives the class a responding-to-literature **prompt** to write about. Shane finishes a details sheet and writes his paragraph.

Writing Prompt

Tell what the poem "Gutter Ball" is about. Choose your favorite part and tell how it makes you feel.

Gutter Ball

I went bowling yesterday.
My ball went down the gutter.
I almost went along with it.
My feet slid, like on butter.

My fingers stuck inside the holes.
The big ball weighed a ton.
I wonder when I'm big someday,
If bowling will be fun.

—J.R. Taylor

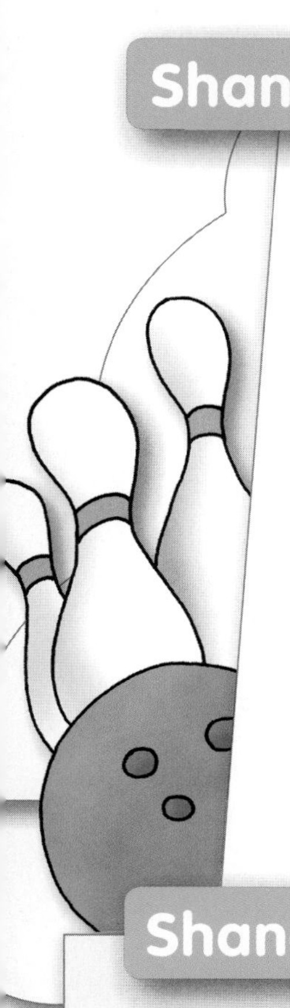

Shane's Details Sheet

1. What is the poem about?
   bowling
2. What is your favorite line or part?
   feet sliding like on butter
3. Why do you like this line or part?
   It makes me think of sliding on my kitchen floor.

Shane's Paragraph

"Gutter Ball"

The poem is about bowling. I like the part about the feet sliding like on butter. It makes me think of sliding on my kitchen floor.

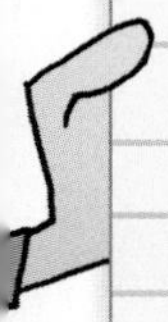

WRITE SOURCE Online
www.hmheducation.com/writesource

Creative Writing

Academic Vocabulary

Work with a partner. Read the meanings and share answers to the questions.

1. You can use your **imagination** to picture new things in your mind. **Close your eyes and think about a day at the beach. What does your imagination picture in your mind?**
2. If words are **repeated** they are written over and over. **What do you read with words that are repeated?**

In **creative writing,** you use words and your imagination to write stories and poems.

Literature Connections: You can find an example of creative writing in *A Cupcake Party* by David McPhail.

Writing Stories

Reading or listening to stories is fun. With some planning, you can write your own made-up stories.

Kaylee writes her story.

Kaylee likes to make up stories of her own. She likes to write about animals.

This chapter will show you how to write a story, too. Remember these points when you write a story.

1. You include characters, a setting, a problem, and a plot.

2. You write a beginning, a middle, and an ending.

Look at the parts of a story.

Characters

The **characters** are the people or animals in the story.

Setting

The **setting** tells when and where the story happens.

Problem

The **problem** is the trouble the main characters face.

Plot

The **plot** is what happens when the characters try to solve the problem.

Suzi's Missing Hiss

One morning, Suzi the snake woke up. Something was wrong. Suzi could not hiss. She twirled around. She stood on her head. She even tied herself in a knot. Nothing worked. Suzi still couldn't hiss. So she went to see Dr. Owl. He hooted, "You have a cold! Go to bed." Suzi slept and slept. She woke up and hissed a tiny, soft hiss. Then she smiled and hissed a big, loud hiss!

Beginning

The **beginning** names the main character and the setting. It also tells about the problem.

Middle

The **middle** tells how the main character tries to solve the problem.

Ending

The **ending** tells how the problem is solved and how the main character feels.

Talk about it.

1. Who is the main character in this story?
2. What is the problem?
3. How is the problem solved?

Prewrite ▸ Plan your story.

Carlo prewrites to plan his story. First, Carlo lists animals he likes. Then he chooses his main character and makes a story plan.

lion

eagle

crab

whale

Herman
morning
lost shell

Beginning

small big

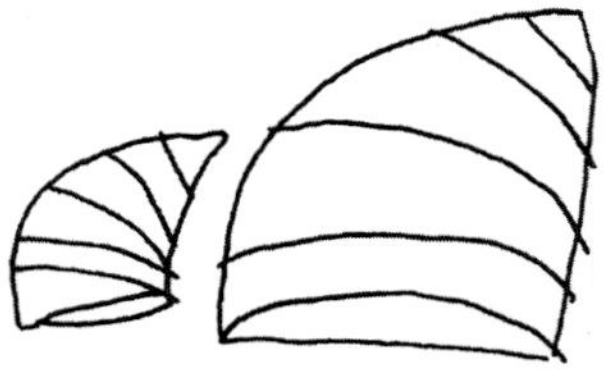

Middle

just right

Ending

Prewrite

Plan your story.

1. **List** animals and **choose** your main character.
2. **Make** your story plan.

Write ▸ Write your first draft.

Carlo uses the ideas from his story plan to write sentences. This is his first draft.

One morning, Herman the crab was exrcizing and had a surprise. His shell popped off and rolled into the ocean. Tasha the turtle said, "Try on other shells." Some shells were too small. They pinched. One shell was too big Herman was getting tired. He saw a shiny shell. He tried it on. it was just right.

Write

Write your first draft.

1. **Use** the ideas in your story plan.
2. **Write** sentences to make a first draft.

Revise and Edit ▸ Make changes.

Carlo reads his story to a partner. He makes changes and checks for conventions.

One morning, Herman the crab
exercising Oops!
was exrcizing and had a surprise.^His
shell popped off and rolled into the
ocean. Tasha the turtle said, "Try
on other shells." Some shells were too
small. They pinched. One shell was too
big. Herman was getting tired.
Then h I
^He saw a shiny shell. He tried it on. it
Herman liked his new home.
was just right.^

Revise and Edit

Make changes and check your story.

1. **Read** your story to a partner.
2. **Change** your story to make it better.
3. **Check** capital letters, end marks, and spelling.

Publish ▸ Share your writing.

Carlo adds a title to his story and makes a neat final copy. He shares his story with another class.

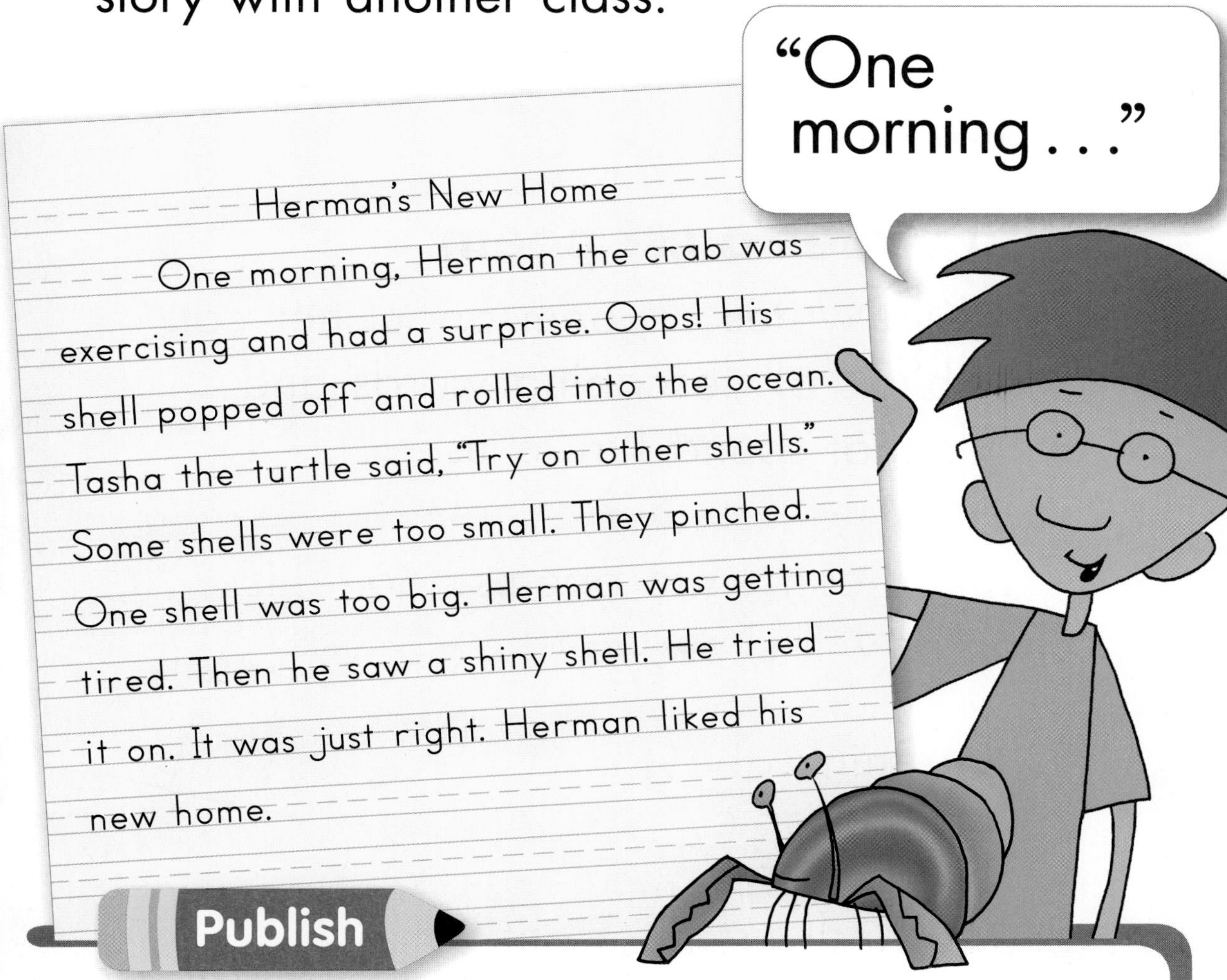
Herman's New Home

One morning, Herman the crab was exercising and had a surprise. Oops! His shell popped off and rolled into the ocean. Tasha the turtle said, "Try on other shells." Some shells were too small. They pinched. One shell was too big. Herman was getting tired. Then he saw a shiny shell. He tried it on. It was just right. Herman liked his new home.

Share your writing.

1. **Add** a title to your story.
2. **Make** a neat final copy of your story.
3. **Read** your story to others.

Writing Poems

Writing poems is like making pictures with words. A list poem is a special type of poem. It follows a pattern.

Kita writes a list poem.

Kita writes a poem about her cat. She thinks of describing words and words that sound fun to use.

You can write poems, too. This chapter will show you how.

1. You think about a special topic.

2. You find just the right describing words to share your ideas.

Kita's Poem

Cats

Cats are curious.
Cats are snuggly.
Cats are sneaky.
Cats are furry.
Cats are purry.
Cats are curious!

Talk about it.

1. What describing words does Kita use to tell about cats?
2. Which words are repeated?
3. Which sentence starts and ends the poem?

Prewrite ▸ Plan your writing.

Aaron talks to others about topics. He looks in his notebook, too. Finally, he chooses one topic for his poem. Then Aaron makes a cluster of describing words to gather details.

Aaron's Cluster

Prewrite

Choose a topic and gather details.

1. **Choose** your topic.
2. **Gather** details about the topic in a cluster.

Write ▸ Write your first draft.

Aaron writes his first draft. He puts his ideas on paper. The pattern of his poem is a list of sentences that begin the same way.

Write your first draft.

1. **Begin** each sentence the same way.
2. **Add** a new describing word to each sentence.
3. **End** your poem with your first sentence.

Revise and Edit ▸ Make changes.

Aaron revises and edits his poem. First, he reads his poem. Then he makes a change and checks his poem for conventions.

Revise and Edit

Make changes and check your poem.

1. **Change** the order of your sentences if you wish.
2. **Check** your writing for capital letters, end marks, and spelling.

Publish ▸ Share your writing.

Aaron publishes his poem. He makes a neat final copy, adds a title, and shares it with others.

Silly Spaghetti

Spaghetti is messy.
Spaghetti is slurpy.
Spaghetti is slippery.
Spaghetti is sloppy.
Spaghetti is messy.

Publish

Share your writing.

1. **Make** a neat final copy of your poem.
2. **Add** a title and a drawing.
3. **Read** your poem to others.

Try other kinds of poems.

ABC Poem

An **ABC poem** uses part of the alphabet to make a list poem.

Jump
Kick
Look at
Me
Now.

Rhyming Poem

My red shoes are really fast.
Ready, set, go! I zoom past!

A **rhyming poem** uses words that rhyme at the ends of the lines.

WRITE SOURCE Online
www.hmheducation.com/writesource

Report Writing

Academic Vocabulary

Work with a partner. Read the meanings and share answers to the questions.

1. If you have **information** about a thing, you know something about it.
   Where can you find information about how to spell words?
2. **Web** is short for World Wide Web.
   On the computer, you can find out news and information using the Web. What would you like to learn about on the Web?

When you write a report, you share factual information. You share what you have learned about a topic.

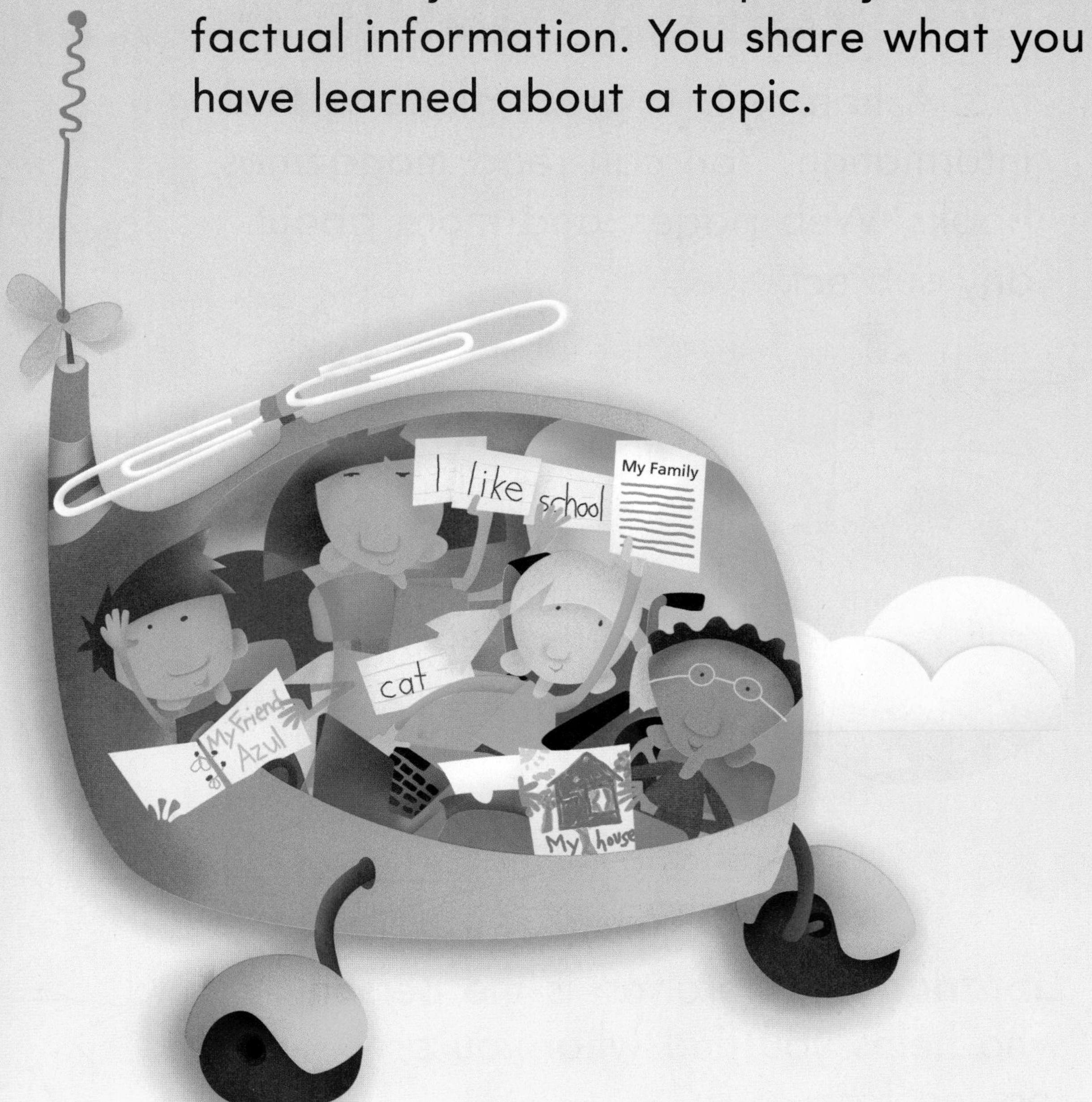

Literature Connections: Like a report, *Amazing Animals* by Gwendolyn Hooks includes interesting information.

Finding Information

A library is a great place to find information. You can read magazines, books, Web pages, and more about any subject.

Books Some books are small, and some books are big. Some are fiction, and some are nonfiction. Some books are all pictures.

Librarian The librarian is the person who helps you find what you are looking for.

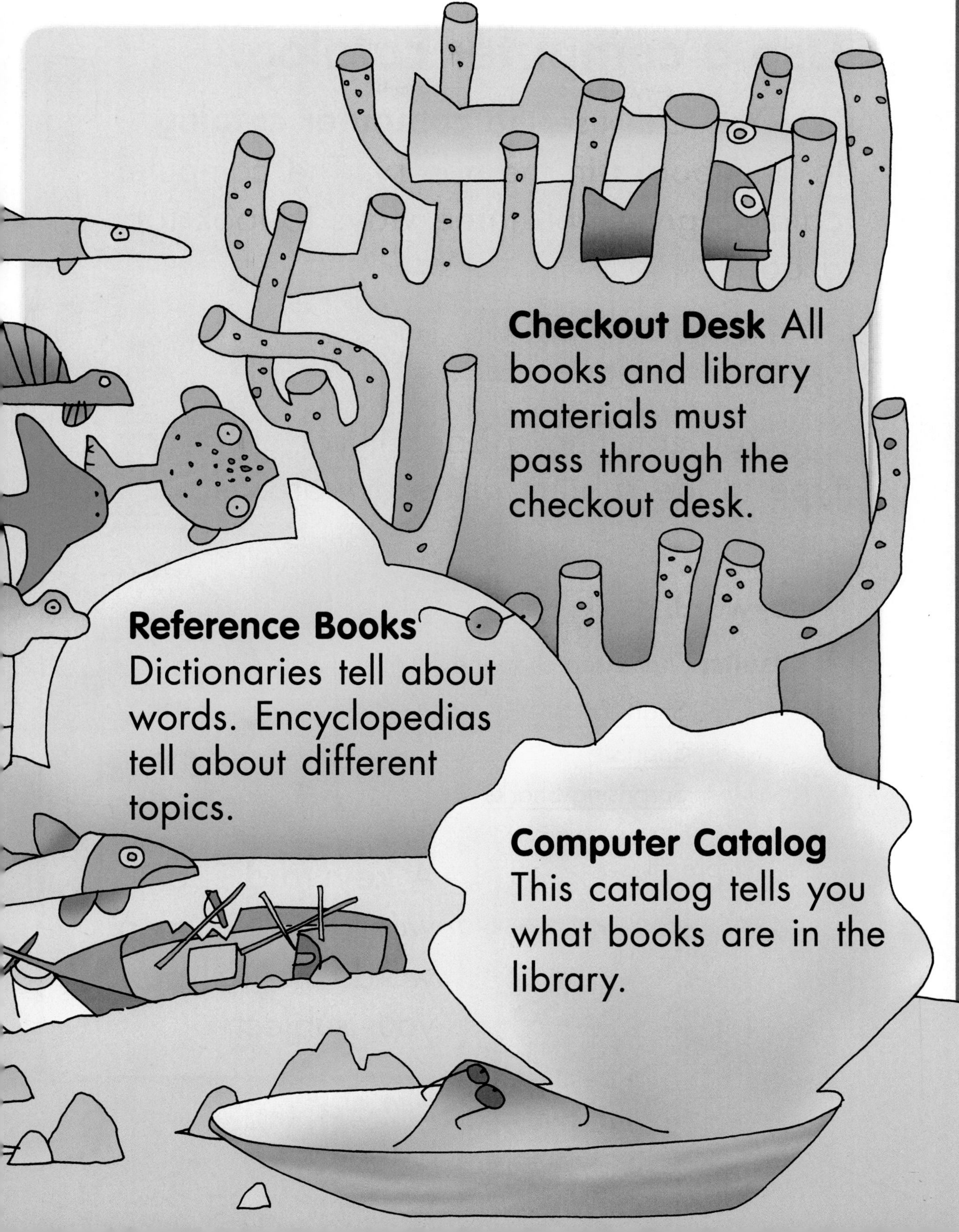

Checkout Desk All books and library materials must pass through the checkout desk.

Reference Books
Dictionaries tell about words. Encyclopedias tell about different topics.

Computer Catalog
This catalog tells you what books are in the library.

Use a computer catalog.

You can use the **computer catalog** to find books in the library. The computer catalog gives you three ways to look for a book.

Search for a subject.

You can find a book if you type in the subject or a keyword.

Keyword: Sharks

Results: *Sharks* search found 10 titles.

Shark Facts

Sharks

Surprising Sharks

more titles >>>

Search for a title.

You can find a book if you type in its title.

Title: Shark Facts

Author: Shaw, Marie.

Publisher: Daniels Press, 2009

Pages: 32

Notes: This book tells about kinds of sharks, where sharks live, and what sharks eat.

Subjects: sharks, ocean life

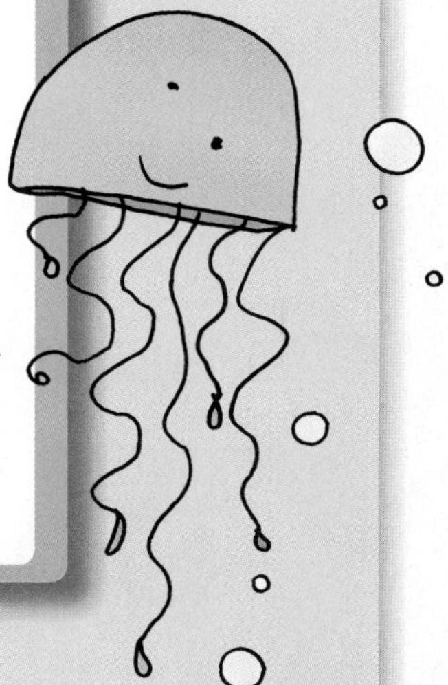

Search for an author.

You can find a book if you type in the name of the author.

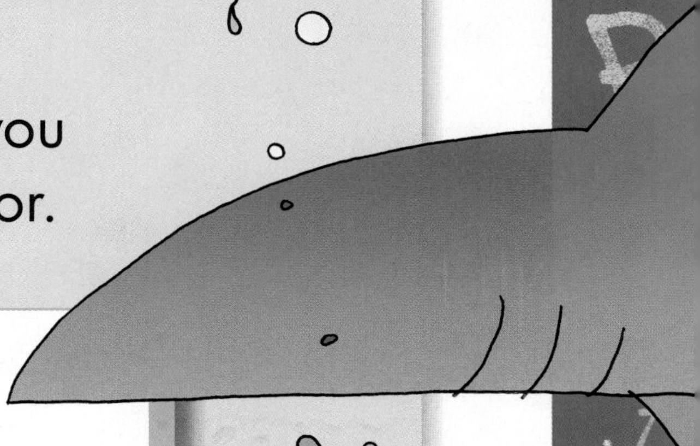

Author: Shaw, Marie

Results: 3

Beautiful Butterflies
Shark Facts
Tigers and Other Big Cats

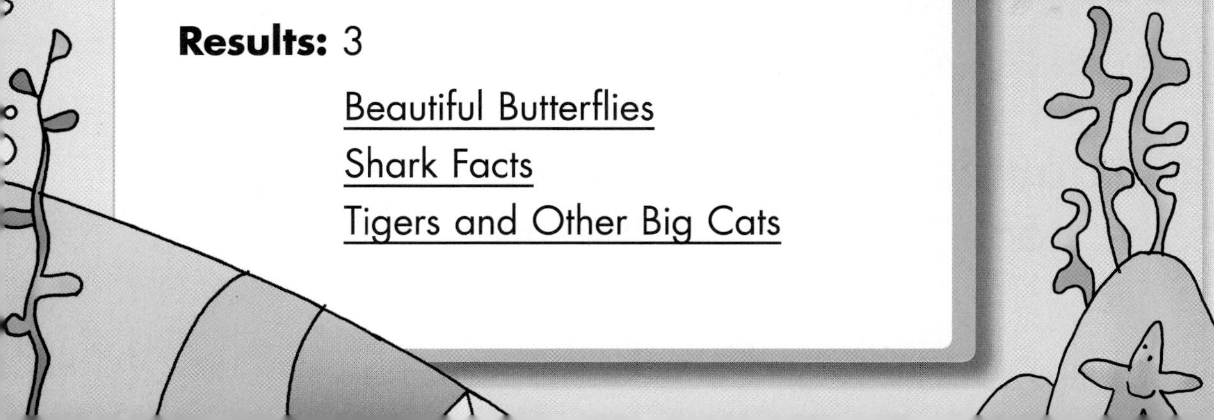

Learn the parts of a book.

Books have special parts. The cover identifies the book. Other parts help the reader find information in the book.

Look at the cover.

The **title** names the book.

The **author** wrote the book.

The **illustrator** made the pictures.

Look inside the book.

Table of Contents

The page numbers and chapters are listed in the front of the book.

Contents

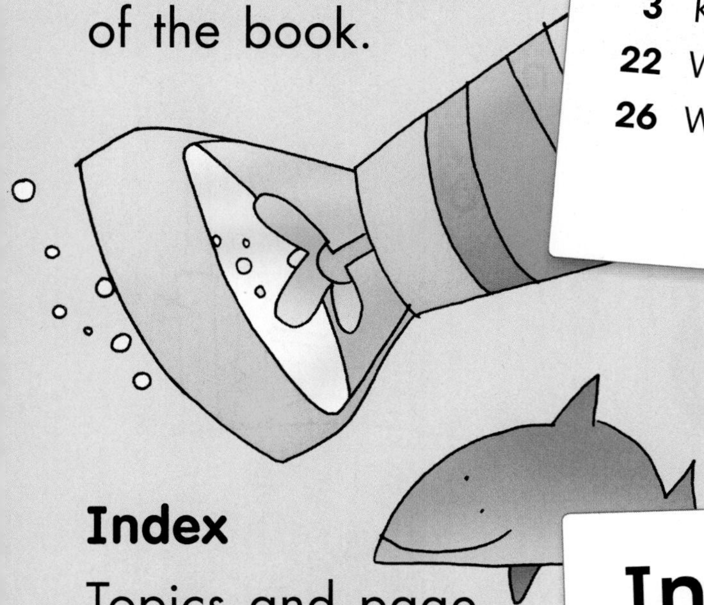

Index

Topics and page numbers are listed in ABC order in the back of the book.

Index

Using a Dictionary

A **dictionary** is a book that helps you learn about words. You use a dictionary to check your spelling. You use it to find the meaning of a word. All of the entry words are in ABC order.

Sample Dictionary Page

9

Aa apple—astronaut

apple An **apple** is a kind of fruit. Apples may be red, green, or yellow.

*This **apple** tastes sweet.*

arm The **arm** is one part of the body. It is between the hand and the shoulder.

*My **arm** was in a cast for six weeks.*

astronaut An **astronaut** is a person who goes into space.

*An **astronaut** wears a special suit.*

This is an **entry word**.

The **meaning** of the word follows the entry word.

apple An **apple** is a kind of fruit. Apples may be red, green, or yellow.

This ***apple*** *tastes sweet.*

A **sentence** helps you understand the word.

A **picture** shows you the meaning.

Talk about it.

Name two other entry words shown on the sample dictionary page.

Writing a Report

In a report, you share facts and information about a topic.

Jake writes a report.

Jake writes a report about an unusual animal that he saw at an aquarium. You can write a report, too. This chapter will show you how.

Jake's Report

Leafy Sea Dragon

The leafy sea dragon is unusual. It looks like a sea horse with green and yellow leaves.

It lives in the ocean by Australia. It hides in kelp forests. Kelp is giant seaweed.

The sea dragon eats tiny shrimp and small fish. It uses its mouth like a straw.

The father sea dragon takes care of the babies. He keeps them in a pouch on his body.

Prewrite ▸ Plan your report.

Before you write a report, you choose a topic and gather details about it. The facts you find are called **details**.

Choose From the class list, Jake chooses the leafy sea dragon for his topic.

Read He reads about it.

Answer He answers the questions on his gathering grid.

Jake's Gathering Grid

Gathering Grid

Topic: leafy sea dragon

1. What does the animal look like? sea horse green and yellow leaves	**2.** Where does it live? kelp forests ocean Australia
3. What does it eat? tiny shrimp small fish uses mouth like a straw	**4.** What are other interesting facts? father takes care of the babys pouch on his body

Prewrite

Choose your topic and gather details.

1. **Choose** an animal.
2. **Read** about it.
3. **Answer** questions on a gathering grid.

Write ▸ Write your beginning.

When you write a report, you put facts about your topic into sentences.

Here is what Jake does to write his beginning paragraph.

Use Jake uses details from his gathering grid.

Introduce He introduces his topic in the first sentence.

Answer Then he answers the first question on his gathering grid.

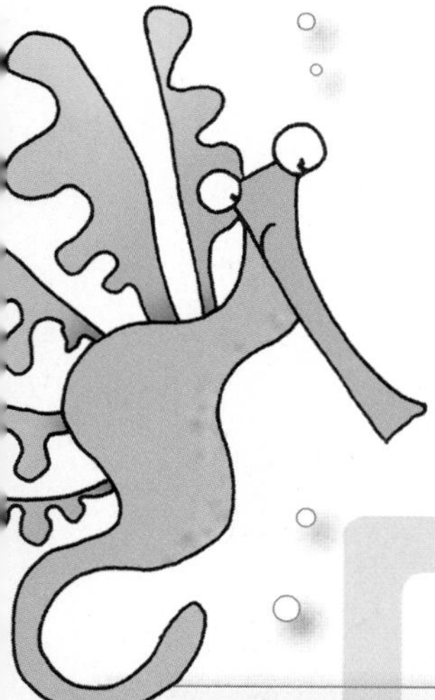

Gathering Grid

Topic: **leafy sea dragon**

1. What does the animal look like?	2. Where does it live?
sea horse **green and yellow leaves**	**kelp forests** **ocean** **Australia**

The leafy sea dragon is unusual. It looks like green and yellow leaves.

Write

Write your beginning paragraph.

1. **Use** your gathering grid.
2. **Introduce** your topic in the first sentence.
3. **Answer** the first question on your gathering grid.

Write ▶ Finish your first draft.

Next, you write the rest of the paragraphs with facts about your topic.

Here is what Jake does to write the rest of his first draft.

Follow Jake follows the order of his gathering grid.

Write He writes a paragraph to answer each question.

Gathering Grid

Topic: leafy sea dragon

1. What does the animal look like?	2. Where does it live?
sea horse green and yellow leaves	kelp forests ocean Australia
3. What does it eat?	**4. What are other interesting facts?**
tiny shrimp small fish uses mouth like a straw	father takes care of the babys pouch on his body

It lives in the ocean by Australia it hides in kelp forests.

The sea dragon eats tiny shrimp and small fish. It uses its mouth like a straw.

The father sea dragon takes care of the babys. He keeps them in a pouch.

Write

Finish your first draft.

1. **Follow** the order of your gathering grid.
2. **Write** a paragraph to answer each question.

Revise ▶ **Change your report.**

When you revise, you make changes to your report.

Here is what Jake does to revise his first draft.

Read Jake reads his first draft.

Add He adds details.

Jake's Revising

The leafy sea dragon is unusual. It

a sea horse with

looks like ^ green and yellow leaves.

It lives in the ocean by Australia it

Kelp is giant seaweed.

hides in kelp forests. ^

The sea dragon eats tiny shrimp and small fish. It uses its mouth like a straw.

The father sea dragon takes care of

on his body

the babys. He keeps them in a pouch ^.

Revise

Make changes to your report.

1. **Read** your first draft.
2. **Add** more details.

Edit ▸ Change your writing.

When you edit your report, you check for capital letters, end marks, and spelling.

Here is what Jake does to check his writing.

Read Jake reads his revised copy.

Check He checks his capital letters, end marks, and spelling.

Correct He corrects any errors.

Jake's Editing

The leafy sea dragon is unusual. It
a sea horse with
looks like ^ green and yellow leaves.

I
It lives in the ocean by Australia. it
Kelp is giant seaweed.
hides in kelp forests. ^

The sea dragon eats tiny shrimp and small fish. It uses its mouth like a straw.

The father sea dragon takes care
babies on his body
of the babys. He keeps them in a pouch ^

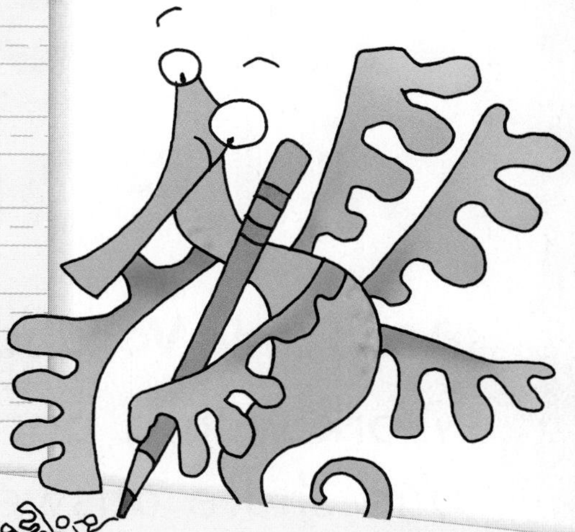

Leafy Sea Dragon

The leafy sea dragon is unusual. It looks like a sea horse with green and yellow leaves.

It lives in the ocean by Australia. It hides in kelp forests. Kelp is giant seaweed.

The sea dragon eats tiny shrimp and small fish. It uses its mouth like a straw.

The father sea dragon takes care of the babies. He keeps them in a pouch on his body.

Edit

Check your writing.

Use the checklist to edit your report.

Publish

Share your writing.

Make a neat final copy of your report. Add drawings, too.

The Tools of Learning

Academic Vocabulary

Work with a partner. Read the meanings and share answers to the questions.

1. When you **choose** something, you take it because it is the one you want.
   How do you choose which clothes to wear?
2. A **viewer** is a person who watches something such as TV or a video.
   How could you be a careful viewer?

In this section, you will learn how to be a careful viewer and a good listener. You will also learn how to do an interview and keep a journal. These speaking and learning skills will help you to become a better student.

Speaking to Others

You can show your classmates a special treasure. You can tell them about a pretty shell, an unusual coin, or a shiny rock.

Here are some rules that you can follow when you talk to your classmates.

Look at your classmates.

Speak loudly and slowly.

Show what you have.

Share important ideas.

When you have something to share, hold it up so that everyone can see it.

Learning to Listen

Listening is an important way to learn at home and at school.

Here are some rules that you can follow to help you listen to parents, teachers, and friends.

Sit quietly or **stand** still.

Look at the person who is talking.

Listen for important words.

Ask any questions after the person stops talking.

If needed, **draw** pictures or write notes about what you hear.

Learning to Interview

In an **interview**, you ask someone questions. Then you write down what you learn.

You can use this plan whenever you do an interview.

First

Before the Interview

Set a time. (Have a grown-up help you.)

Think of questions to ask (*why*, *how*, and *what*).

Write down your questions.

Take your questions, a pencil, and paper to the interview.

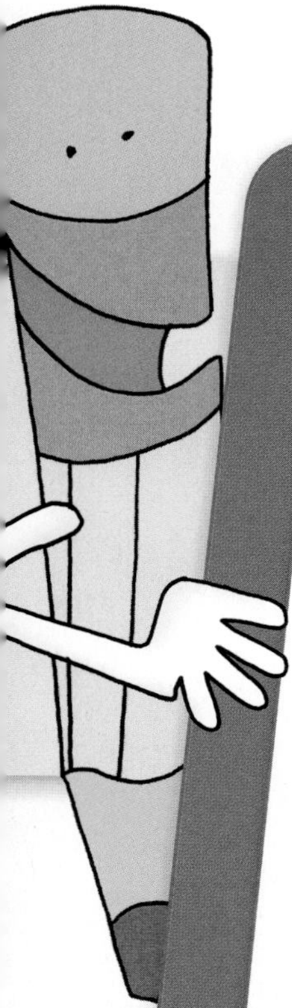

Next

During the Interview

Ask one question at a time.

Listen carefully to the answer.

Write an answer for each question.

Thank the person.

Last

After the Interview

Write about what you learned.

Writing in Journals

A **journal** is a special notebook. You can write about all kinds of things in a journal.

Here are some ideas to write about in your journal.

In your journal, you can write poems, jokes, and stories. You can describe places and list questions you have.

April 6

I had fun yesterday. I rode my bike through some puddles. The tires made tracks on the sidewalk.

Use a special notebook.

Write the date each time you write in your journal.

Tell about what you see and do.

Share your thoughts and your feelings.

Draw pictures if you wish.

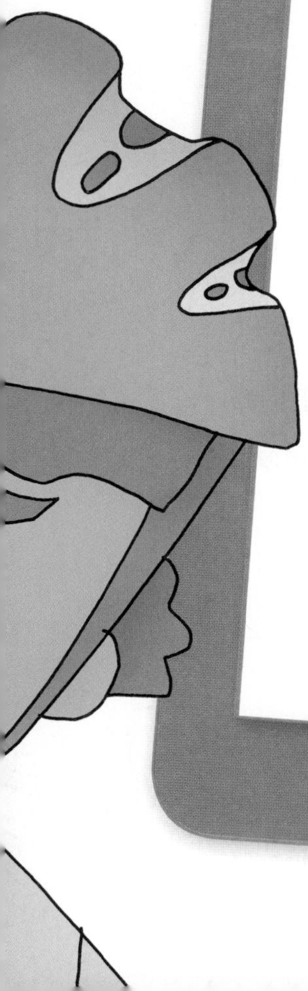

Using Learning Logs

A **learning log** is a special kind of journal. You write about facts that you are learning. You ask questions and underline new words.

Here is what you can do when you write in a learning log.

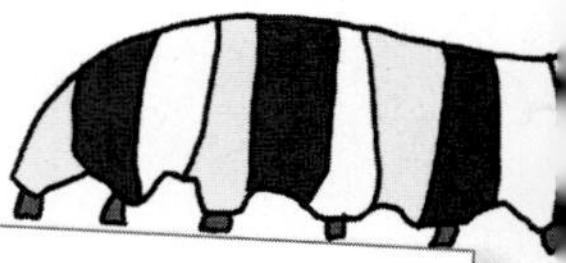

May 4, Science

Sara brought a yellow, white, and black caterpillar to school. Mr. Kane put it in a jar with <u>milkweed</u> leaves.

May 5, Science

The caterpillar eats and eats. Sara adds more leaves every day.

May 18, Science

The fat caterpillar is hanging upside down. Why is it doing that?

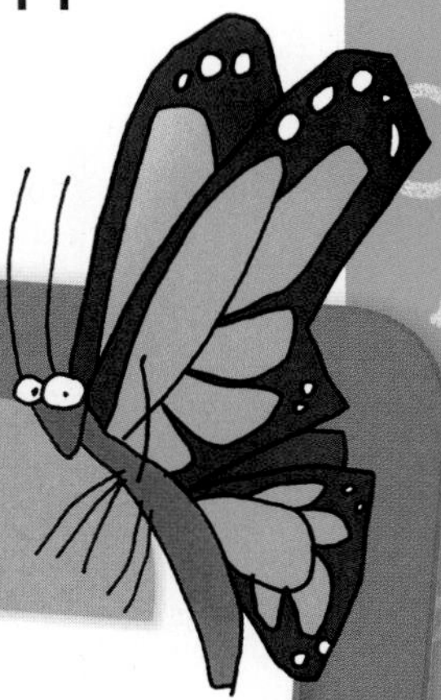

Write the date and the subject.

Tell a new fact you learn or what happens in class.

Share your thoughts about it.

Ask any questions you have.

Underline new words.

May 19, Science

Where did the caterpillar go? Mr. Kane says it is inside the green case with gold dots. It is called a <u>chrysalis</u>.

May 29, Science

Surprise! A monarch butterfly came out of the chrysalis. It pumped its orange and black wings. Sara let it fly outside.

Being a Smart Viewer

Television, videos, and the Internet share information and stories about real people and events. They also show make-believe stories with cartoons and actors.

Here are things to remember when you watch TV, look at a video, or use the Internet.

Ask adults to help you make good choices about what you view.

Remember that commercials and ads are trying to sell you something.

Write down new facts you learn from a show about real people or events.

Share what you have learned.

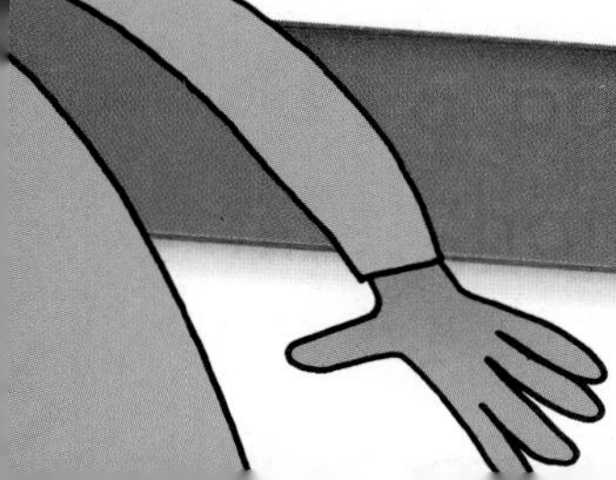

Taking Tests

In school, you learn many new facts and ideas. You study, and then you take tests. A test tells you and your teacher how much you learned.

Matching Test

A **matching test** asks you to choose words that go together.

Read both lists below. Draw a line between the adult animal and the baby animal.

Adult	Baby
1. dog	calf
2. cow	kitten
3. cat	puppy

Multiple-Choice Test

A **multiple-choice test** asks you to choose the best answer.

Fill in the circle next to the correct answer.

1. Kurt had 3 apples. He gave his sister one. How many apples did Kurt have left?

Ⓐ $4-1 = 3$

Ⓑ $3-1 = 2$

Ⓒ $3-2 = 1$

Fill-in-the-Blank Test

A **fill-in-the-blank** test usually asks you to finish a sentence.

Choose and write the best word from the box to finish each sentence.

green	**blue**	**yellow**
orange	**red**	**purple**

1. A stop sign is ___**red**___ and white.
2. The school bus is ___**yellow**___.
3. On a clear day, the sky is ___**blue**___.
4. Mix yellow and blue paint to make **green**.

Short-Answer Test

A **short-answer** test asks you to answer a question. You may write one word, several words, or a short sentence.

Write a word or words to answer each question.

1. What is something white in your desk?

   paper

2. What are two green things outside?

   leaves and grass

3. What are three purple things in the classroom?

   clock

   block

   grapes on the color chart

Words

Academic Vocabulary

Work with a partner. Read the meanings and share answers to the questions.

1. A **person** is a man, woman, or child. **What kind of person is your teacher?**
2. Something that is **happening** is going on or taking place. **What is happening in your classroom right now?**
3. If you **compare** two things, you see how they are different and alike. **How would you compare an apple and an orange?**

Words are used to share your ideas. You use words when you speak and when you write.

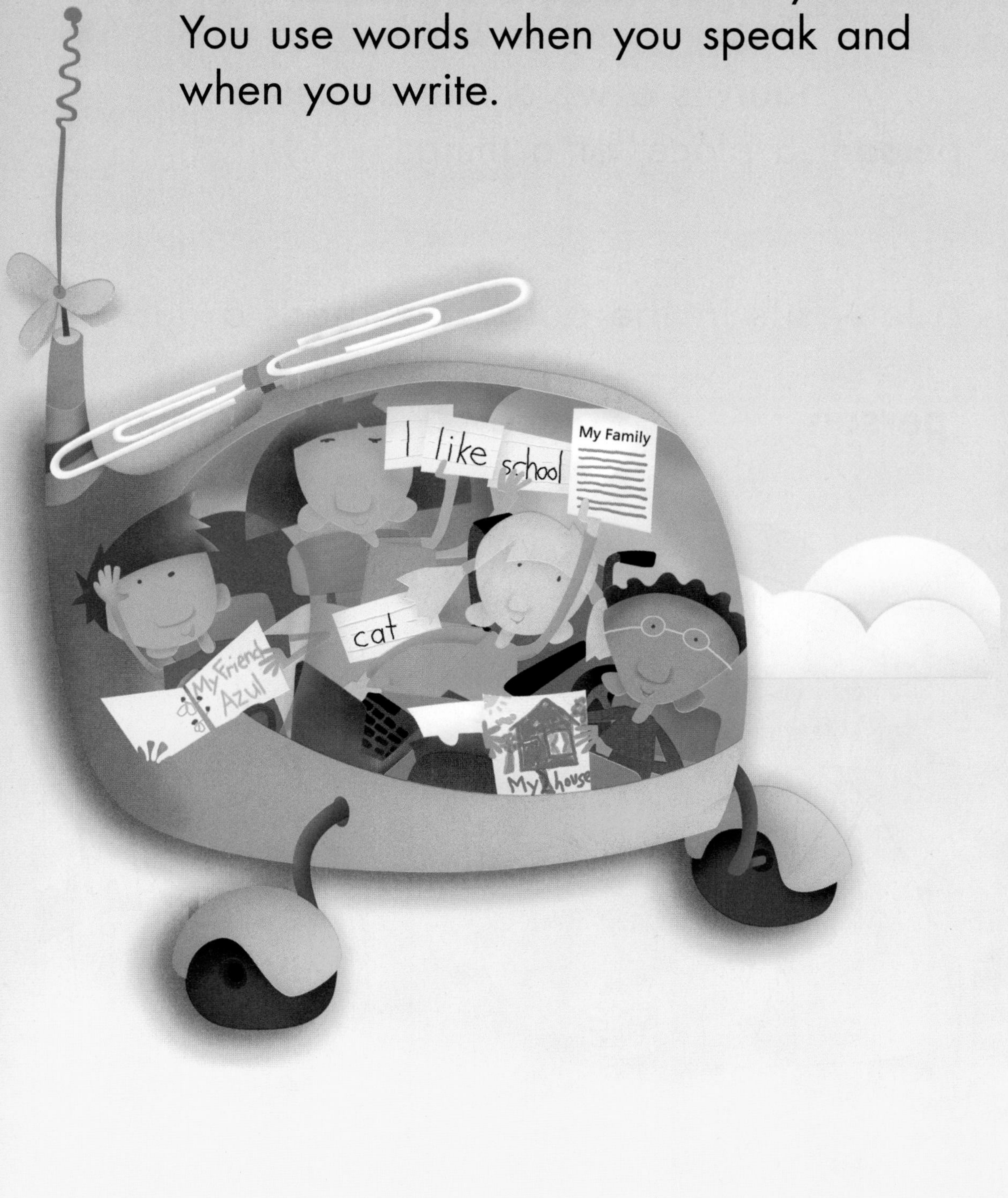

Learning About Nouns

A **noun** is a word that names a person, a place, or a thing.

A lady sits in the park. She feeds a duck.

person **place** **thing**

More Nouns

Person	Place	Thing
boy	farm	rock
girl	store	cat
doctor	zoo	bus
plumber	school	car

Grammar Practice

Read each sentence. Tell if the underlined **noun** names a person, a place, or a thing.

Example: **Our teacher plays the piano.**

1. See the pretty rose.
2. My uncle reads me stories.
3. My dog runs and jumps.
4. Listen to my aunt sing.
5. The library is very quiet.

Common and Proper Nouns

A **common noun** names any person, place, or thing. A **proper noun** names a special person, place, or thing. It begins with a capital letter.

Common Nouns	Proper Nouns
boy	Frank
river	Ohio River
book	The Zoo Book

Grammar Practice

Read the words below. Tell if the word is a **common noun** or a **proper noun**.

Example: **lake, Frog Lake**

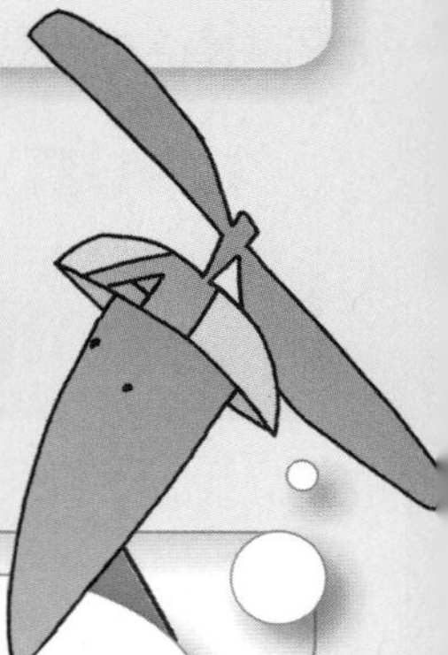

lake—common
Frog Lake—proper

1. family, Watsons
2. sister, Susan
3. Pacific Ocean, ocean

Singular and Plural Nouns

A **singular noun** names one person, place, or thing. A **plural noun** names more than one person, place, or thing. Add **-s** to make most nouns plural.

Singular Nouns	Plural Nouns
girl	girls
garden	gardens
hammer	hammers

Grammar Practice

Spell the plural of each **noun** below.

Example: **snack**

s-n-a-c-k-s

1. kite
2. coat
3. orange
4. nest
5. sock
6. car

Using Pronouns

A **pronoun** is a word that takes the place of a noun. Some common pronouns are *he, she,* and *it.*

Ellen wiggled the tooth.

Ellen wiggled it.

Mike had a loose tooth.

He had a loose tooth.

Grammar Practice

Choose the right **pronoun** for each underlined noun.

Example: **Mom buys a tree.** ***(It, She)***

1. Todd helps Mom plant the tree. *(He, She)*
2. Then Todd waters the tree. *(he, it)*
3. Mom thanks Todd for helping. *(It, She)*

Using *I* and *Me*

I and me are pronouns you use to write about yourself. These pronouns are singular. The word **I** is always capitalized.

Use I as the **naming part,** or **subject,** of the sentence.

I play in our backyard.

Use me after the verb in the **telling part**.

Janey writes me a note.

Grammar Practice

Choose the right **pronoun** for each sentence.

Example: **My aunt gave *(I, me)* a new book.**

1. My friend and *(I, me)* jump rope.
2. Mom sings to my sister and *(I, me).*
3. She and *(I, me)* like tomato soup.

Using *We* and *Us*

We and **us** are pronouns you use to write about others and yourself. These pronouns are plural.

Use **we** as the **subject** of the sentence.

We have gym every Friday.

Use **us** after the **verb**.

Our teacher shows us new games.

Grammar Practice

Choose the right **pronoun** for each sentence.

Example: ***(We, Us)*** **had fun in science today.**

1. Mr. King told *(we, us)* about sound waves.
2. *(We, Us)* made waves with string and spoons.
3. He gave *(we, us)* jars full of water.

Using *They* and *Them*

They and **them** are pronouns you use to write about others. These pronouns are plural.

Use **they** as the **subject** of the sentence.

They **bake bread every week.**

Use **them** after the **verb**.

Nana helps them **get ready.**

Grammar Practice

Choose the right **pronoun** for each sentence.

Example: ***(They, Them)* wash their hands.**

1. Nana gives *(they, them)* directions.
2. *(They, Them)* each knead the dough.
3. Nana bakes the bread for *(they, them).*
4. Finally, *(they, them)* eat the warm bread.

Learning About Verbs

A **verb** is a word that shows action or helps complete a thought. An **action verb** tells what is happening.

Action Verbs

Turtles crawl.

The snake slithers.

Grammar Practice

Choose an **action verb** from the box to finish each sentence.

swim	hoots	spin	fly

Example: **Birds ________ in the sky.**

1. Fish ________ in the water.
2. An owl ________ at night.
3. Spiders ________ webs.

Using Action Verbs

An **action verb** tells what the naming part of the sentence does.

Naming Part	Action Verb
The seal	barks.
Bears	hunt.

Grammar Practice

makes

Name the **action verb** in each sentence.

Example: **Wen makes a picture.**

1. Wen studies the forest.
2. She draws many trees.
3. She colors the leaves red and yellow.
4. Wen gives her picture to a friend.
5. Her friend says, "Thank you."

Present-Tense Action Verbs

A **present-tense verb** tells what is happening now.

Present-Tense Verbs

Fido barks at a squirrel.

The children chase Fido.

Grammar Practice

Read each sentence. Choose the **action verb** that tells what is happening now.

Example: **A spider *(drops, dropped)* down.**

1. It *(lands, landed)* on my friend.
2. He *(yells, yelled)*, "Oh!"
3. He *(hops, hopped)* around.
4. Finally, I *(brush, brushed)* it off.

Past-Tense Action Verbs

A **past-tense verb** tells what has already happened. Most past-tense verbs end with **-ed**.

Past-Tense Verbs

Fido barked at a squirrel.

The children chased Fido.

Grammar Practice

Read each sentence. Choose the **action verb** that tells what has already happened.

Example: **A chipmunk *(chatters, chattered)*.**

1. The chipmunk *(races, raced)* by me.
2. It *(picks, picked)* up some seeds.
3. The chipmunk *(fills, filled)* its cheeks.
4. It *(stores, stored)* the seeds in its burrow.

Present-Tense Linking Verbs

Linking verbs help complete a thought. The linking verbs *am, is,* and *are* are **present tense**. *Am* and *is* are singular. *Are* is plural.

Present-Tense Linking Verbs

I am seven years old.

Sara is my sister.

Jim and Seth are friends.

Grammar Practice

Name the **linking verb** in each sentence.

Example: **I am a first grader.**

1. Ice is hard and cold.
2. Pillows and feathers are soft.
3. I am a good singer.

Past-Tense Linking Verbs

The linking verbs *was* and *were* are **past tense**. *Was* is singular. *Were* is plural.

Past-Tense Linking Verbs

My brother was excited.

My parents were surprised.

Grammar Practice

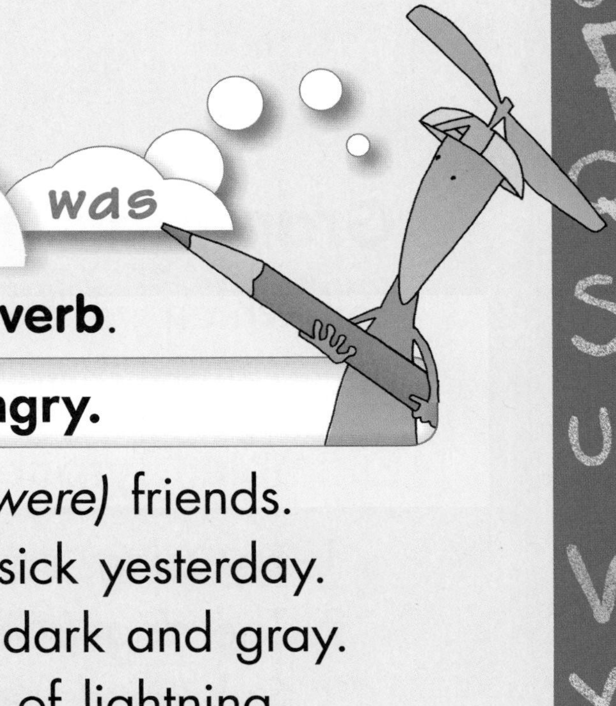

Choose the correct **linking verb**.

Example: **I *(was, were)* hungry.**

1. Christa and Jan *(was, were)* friends.
2. My puppy *(was, were)* sick yesterday.
3. The clouds *(were, was)* dark and gray.
4. The sky *(was, were)* full of lightning.

Singular Subjects and Verbs

The subject and verb in a sentence must agree. That means if the subject is singular, the verb usually ends with an **-s**.

	Singular Subject	Verb + s
one person →	Kaylee	dances.
one place →	The ocean	roars.
one thing →	The monkey	swings.

Grammar Practice

Tell which verb agrees with the underlined subject in each sentence.

Example: **<u>Tyrone</u> *(play, plays)* basketball.**

1. <u>Ivy</u> *(sing, sings)* at home.
2. The <u>dog</u> *(run, runs)* with Mark.
3. <u>Sal</u> *(read, reads)* about dinosaurs.

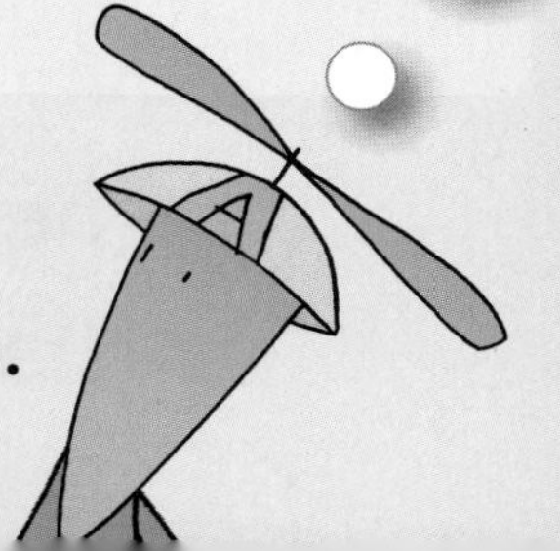

Plural Subjects and Verbs

If the subject is plural, the verb usually does not end with an **-s**.

	Plural Subject	Verb
people →	Kaylee and Lynn	dance.
places →	The oceans	roar.
things →	The monkeys	swing.

Grammar Practice

Tell which verb agrees with the underlined subject in each sentence.

Example: **Bells** ***(ring, rings).***

1. The children *(leave, leaves)* the classroom.
2. Their teachers *(say, says)*, "Good-bye."
3. Buses *(pull, pulls)* up to the school.

Contractions

A **contraction** is a word that is usually made from two words. Sometimes a contraction is made from a **pronoun** and a **verb**. An **apostrophe** (') shows that one or more letters are left out.

Pronoun	+	Verb	=	Contraction
I	+	am	=	I'm
it	+	is	=	it's
he	+	is	=	he's

Grammar Practice

Say the **contraction** for each pair of words.

Example: ***(I am)* reading a book.**

1. *(It is)* about Henry the skunk.
2. *(He is)* friends with another skunk.
3. *(I am)* sure you will like this story, too.

Contractions Using *Not*

Some contractions are made from a **verb** and the word **not**.

Verb	+	Not	=	Contraction
is	+	not	=	isn't
do	+	not	=	don't
did	+	not	=	didn't

Grammar Practice

Say the two words that make each **contraction**.

Example: **A dolphin *(isn't)* a fish.**

1. Bottlenose dolphins *(don't)* like cold water.
2. I *(didn't)* know that.
3. A whale *(isn't)* a fish either.
4. These animals *(don't)* breathe underwater.

Using Adjectives

An **adjective** is a word that tells something about a noun.

Adjectives can tell *what kind.*

A huge hippo lives in the zoo.

Adjectives also tell *how many.*

Three hippos stand in the water.

Grammar Practice

Find the **adjective** that tells *what kind* or *how many* for each underlined noun.

Example: **That blue bird is a jay.**

1. Blue jays are about ten inches long.
2. They use sharp beaks to open seeds.
3. Some jays live in shady woods.

Using Adjectives to Compare

Some adjectives are used to compare.

If an adjective compares **two people, places, or things, add -er.**

Jina is taller than Luisa.

If an adjective compares **three or more people, places, or things, add -est.**

Dario is the tallest boy in my class.

Grammar Practice

Choose the right adjective for each sentence.

Example: **Baby bear was the (littler, littlest) bear.**

1. His bowl was *(smaller, smallest)* than Mama's.
2. Papa had the *(bigger, biggest)* chair.
3. Papa also had the *(longer, longest)* bed.

A Writer's Resource

Academic Vocabulary

Work with a partner. Read the meanings and share answers to the questions.

1. When you **finish** something, you come to the end of it.
   What do you do with your homework when you finish it?
2. A **chart** is a drawing that shows information.
   Is information easier to read in a chart? Explain.
3. To **connect** two things means to join them together.
   What might connect one room to another?

If you need help with your writing, turn to this section. You can find a topic idea. There are ways to help you organize your ideas. Have fun making your writing the best it can be.

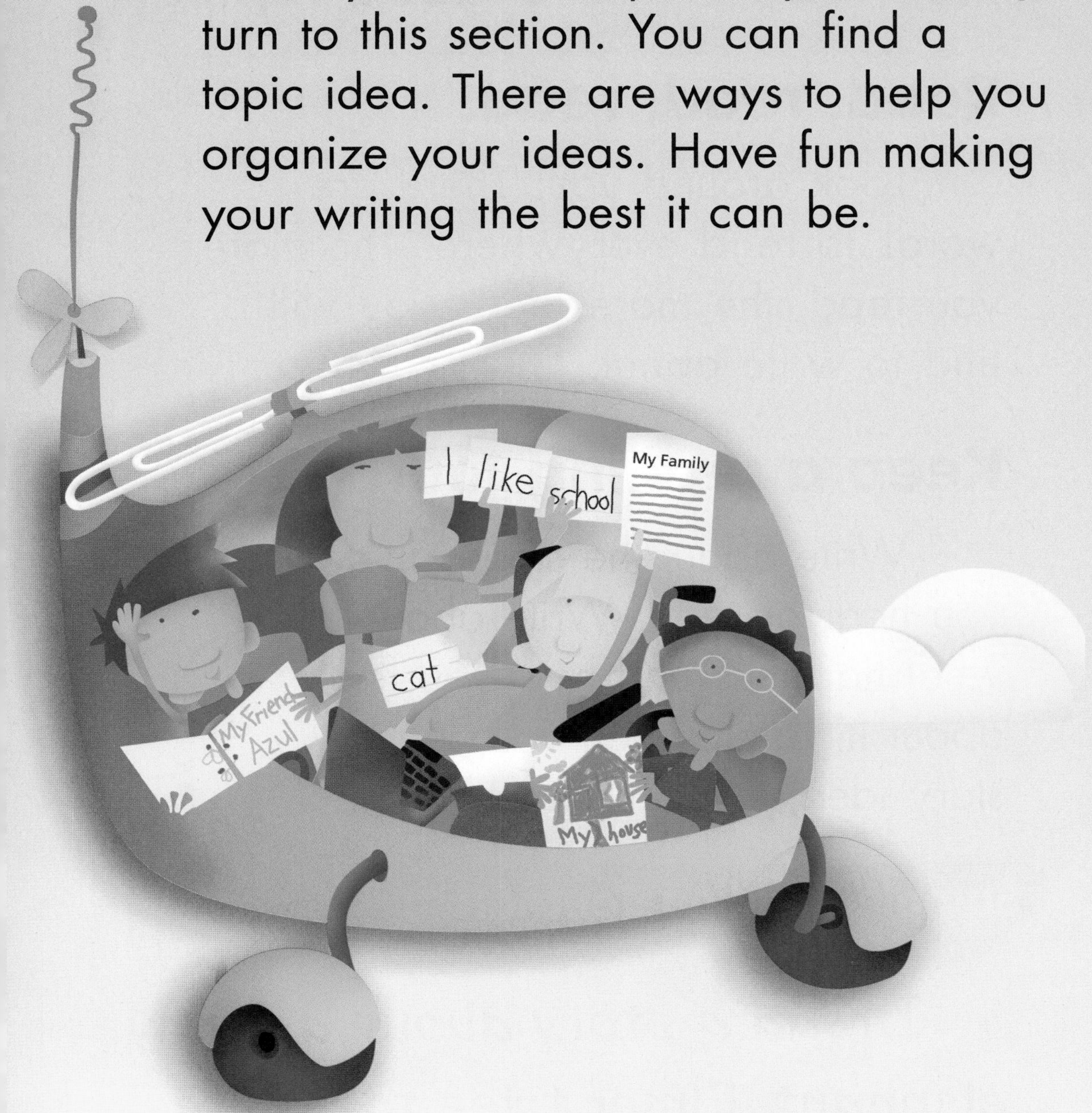

How can I find a good topic?

Read, read, read.

Look around you. There are words to read everywhere. The more you read, the more ideas you will find to write about.

Keep a reading journal.

Write about the stories that you hear or read. Write about what happens and how you feel about it. Later, when you need a story idea, look in your journal.

Sample Reading Journal

I read a story about a funny elephant. Elmer tries to be like everyone else. He learns it is best to be himself.

Make lists.

Write lists of things that you like. Keep the lists in a writer's notebook. When you need a topic, read your list.

Sample Writer's Notebook

Foods	Animals	Places	People
tacos	kittens	beach	Grandpa
yogurt	puppies	zoo	my brother
pancakes	sea lions	school	Mrs. Hall
egg rolls	goldfish	park	Dr. Rice

Finish sentence starters.

Sentence starters can help you think of topics. When you need an idea, finish one of these.

1. Narrative

One time, I ______________________.

Last summer, I ______________________.

2. Descriptive

My bike is ______________________.

A grocery store is ______________________.

3. Expository

A giraffe lives ______________________.

You can learn to ______________________.

4. Persuasive

Everyone should ______________________.

People need to ______________________.

Write in a daily journal.

Write about the things you see and do each day. Read your journal when you need a topic idea.

Daily Journal Entries

April 7, 2011

I heard a loud noise next door. A tractor was pushing dirt around. I wonder why.

April 9, 2011

I watched the workers next door. Mom said they are building a deck. The saws buzzed and the hammers banged. It was loud!

Write about a picture.

A picture can tell a story. Write sentences about what is happening.

Brrr

Henry Hippo wants to go swimming. He puts on his swimsuit. Then he goes to the pond. Henry sticks his big toe in the water. Yikes! The water is too cold. Henry waddles off to play in the sand.

Write about a photograph.

Make up a story about a photograph that you like.

Rat–tat–tat–tat. Rum–tum–a–tum. I march and march with my gold and blue drum. My friends come along. We make our own parade!

How can I organize my ideas?

Make a list.

First, write your topic idea. Then list details about it.

Things I like about swimming

1. *exciting to jump and dive*
2. *cools me off when it's hot*
3. *good exercise*
4. *can swim with friends*
5. *fun to float and watch the sky*

Make a cluster.

Gather details with a cluster, or web. Write your topic in the middle of your paper. Then add details around it.

Make a sensory chart.

List describing words about your topic. Tell what you see, hear, smell, taste, and touch.

Topic: *Grandpa's garage*

see	old car lots of shiny tools
hear	clanging banging rattle
smell	oil gas wood
taste	
touch	greasy rag sticky cobwebs

Make a story map.

Think about a story. Then draw pictures to show the parts of the story in order.

Topic: Goldilocks

Make a 5 W's chart.

Answer the 5 W questions about your topic. Write your answers in a chart. Then use the details from the chart in your writing.

Topic: our librarian

Who?	Miss Gomez
What?	reads us stories
When?	every Tuesday
Where?	in the school library
Why?	to share new books

Make an order chart.

When you want to explain how to do something, list the steps in order. Write a number for each step.

Topic: How to Feed the Dog

Step 1	Put food in one dish.
Step 2	Put fresh water in the other dish.
Step 3	Wipe up any spills.
Step 4	Call the dog.

What is a writing voice?

When you write, it should sound like you are very interested.

Descriptive Voice

Make a picture for the reader by using your five senses.

My red scooter is shiny. It has black handles with silver streamers. The tires go click, click on the sidewalk.

Narrative Voice

Write as if you are telling the story to a friend.

I saw a toad jump in the grass. My dog saw it, too. I grabbed Boxer's collar. The toad was safe!

Expository Voice

Use details to share information or explain an idea.

You can make a sand castle. First, fill a pail with wet sand. Then pat it down. Next, turn the pail over. Lift it very slowly. The sand will come out. Now you have the first tower of your castle wall.

Persuasive Voice

Use good reasons so the reader will agree with you.

The hallway outside our classroom is messy. Kids could trip. We should all hang our coats and backpacks on the hooks outside our room.

How can I learn new words?

Make your own dictionary.

List new words you want to remember in a notebook. Put words that begin with **A** on the **A** page. Put words that begin with **B** on the **B** page. Do the same for every letter.

Personal Dictionary Page

A

apple	Aunt Ann	alligator
Alex	astronaut	almost
are	all	amazing

Use a classroom dictionary.

A dictionary lists words in ABC order. It shows how a word is spelled and tells what it means.

Sample Dictionary Page

Oo **oak—ocean** **25**

oak An **oak** is a kind of tree. Nuts called acorns grow on oak trees.
*The **oak** tree is big.*

ocean An **ocean** is a large body of salt water. Many plants and animals live in the ocean.
*Whales and dolphins live in the **ocean**.*

Use a word bank.

A word bank lists many kinds of words. Look at a word bank, or word wall, to find interesting words. Use these words in your writing.

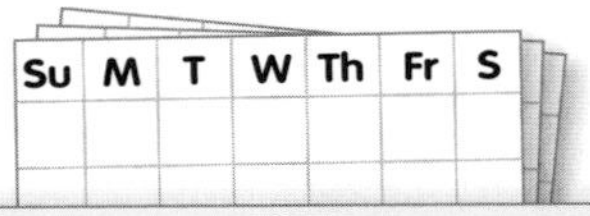

Days	Seasons
Sunday	winter
Monday	spring
Tuesday	summer
Wednesday	fall
Thursday	
Friday	
Saturday	

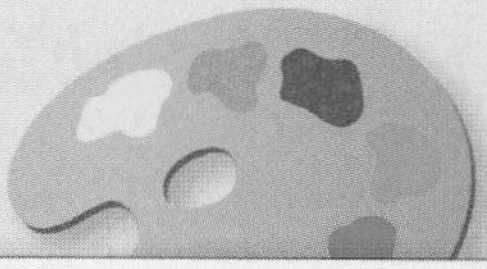

Colors	Numbers	Months
yellow	one	January
green	two	February
blue	three	March
purple	four	April
brown	five	May
black	six	June
white	seven	July
red	eight	August
orange	nine	September
violet	ten	October
		November
		December

How can I connect sentences?

Use time-order words.

Time-order words tell when things happen in a story or report.

Time-Order Word Chart

first second third

yesterday today tomorrow

now then later

first next last

Use place-order words.

Place-order words tell where things are in a description.

Place-Order Word Chart

across	between	on
around	by	outside
behind	inside	over
beside	off	up

What can I add to my writing?

Draw a picture.

Add a picture of a detail from your story or report.

Add a speech bubble.

Beside your picture, write words the character might say.

Add a photo and a caption.

Use a photo to show a special detail about your story. Under the photo, write a few words or a sentence about it. This is called a **caption**.

Photo

Caption

I love to climb.

Add a drawing with labels.

A drawing with labels can make a report clear and interesting.

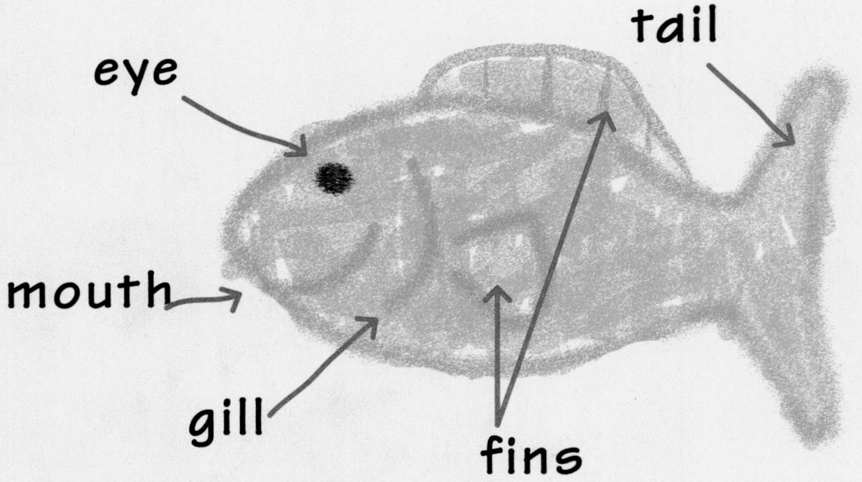

Fish

A fish has special body parts. Each part does a different job. Eyes let a fish see. A fish eats with its mouth. Gills help a fish breathe. A fish swims with its fins and tail.

Add a bar graph.

A **bar graph** can explain numbers in your writing. The graph below shows how many students chose each color as their favorite.

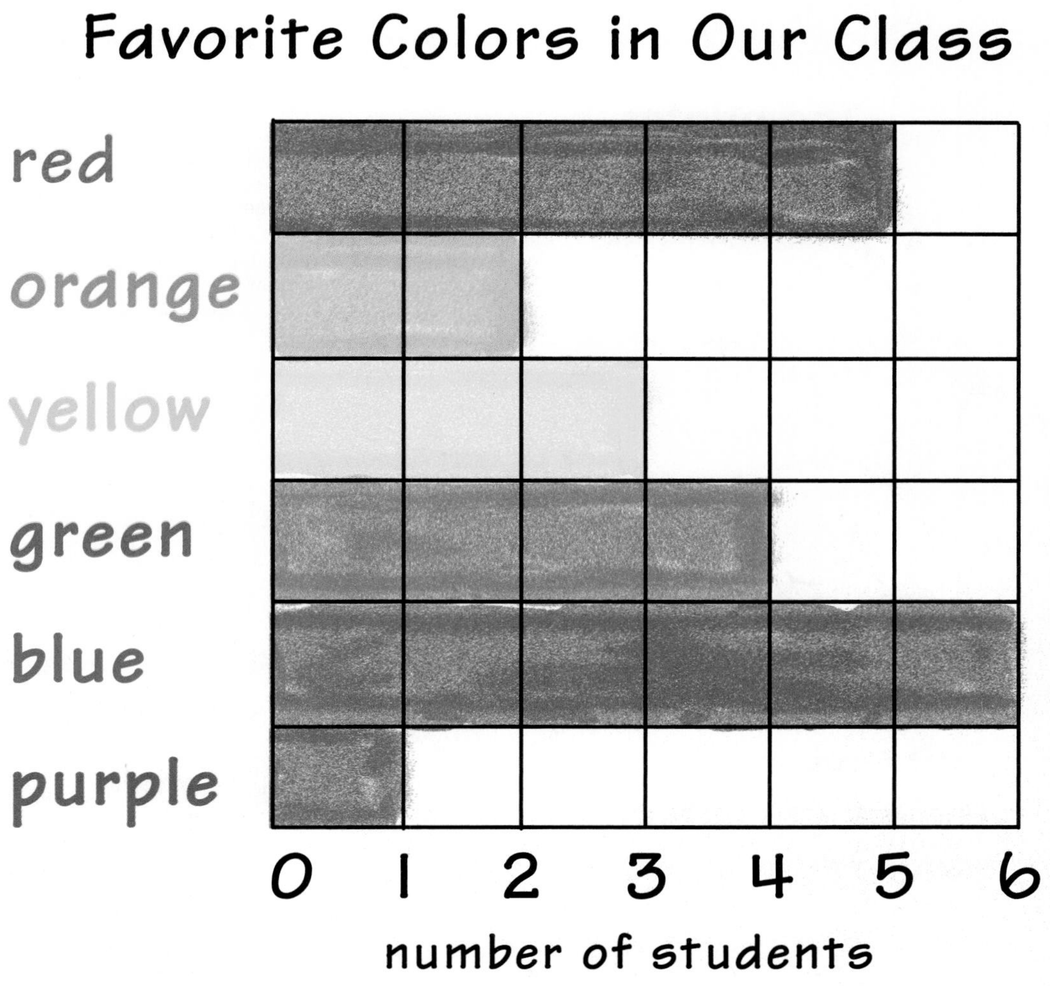

Write on a computer.

The more you know about a computer, the more you can do with it. Try writing on a computer.

Parts of a Computer

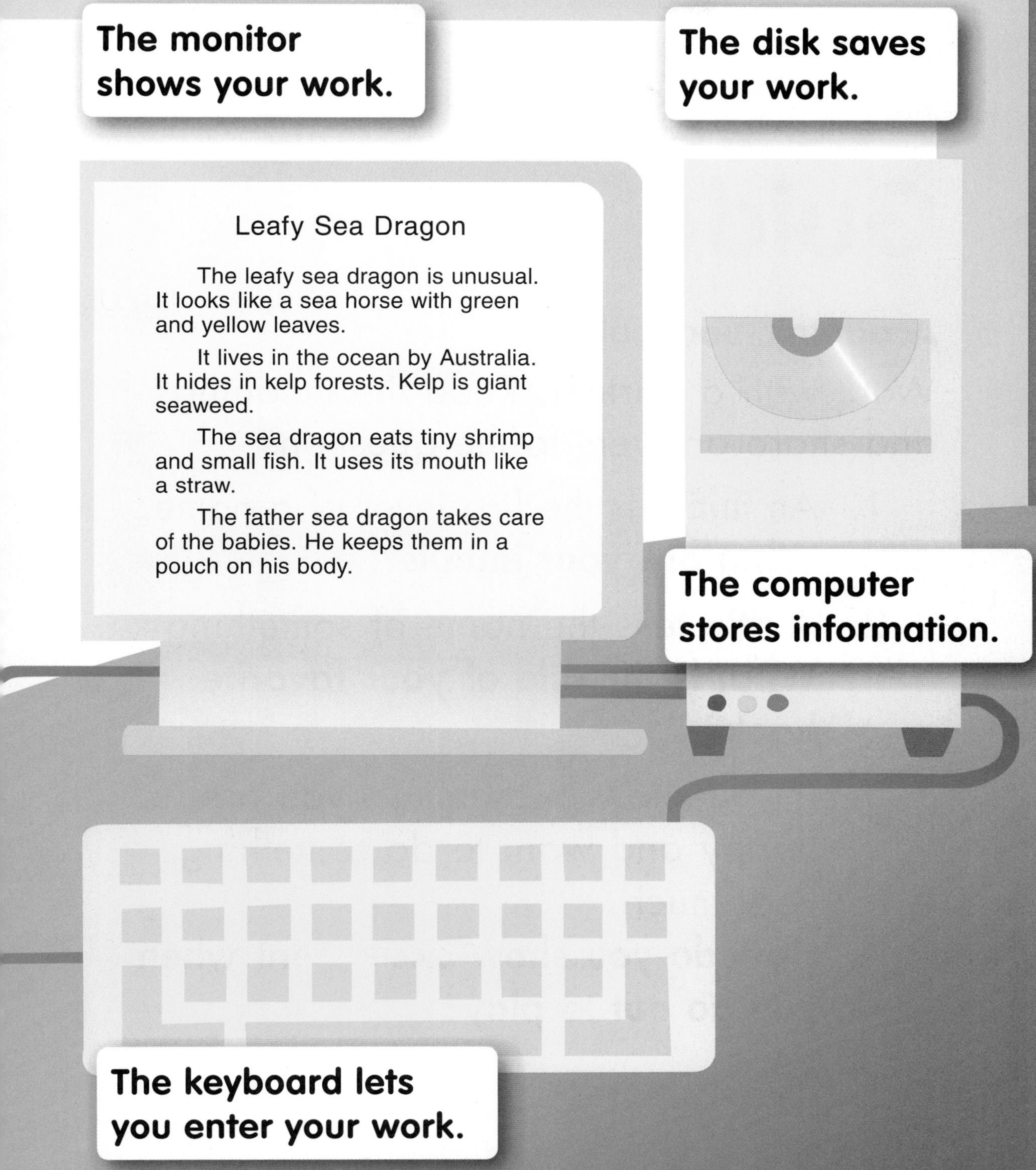
The monitor shows your work.
The disk saves your work.
Leafy Sea Dragon
The leafy sea dragon is unusual. It looks like a sea horse with green and yellow leaves.
It lives in the ocean by Australia. It hides in kelp forests. Kelp is giant seaweed.
The sea dragon eats tiny shrimp and small fish. It uses its mouth like a straw.
The father sea dragon takes care of the babies. He keeps them in a pouch on his body.
The computer stores information.
The keyboard lets you enter your work.

WRITE SOURCE Online
www.hmheducation.com/writesource

Proofreader's Guide

Academic Vocabulary

Work with a partner. Read the meanings and share answers to the questions.

1. An **initial** is the first letter of a name. **What are your initials?**
2. A **title** tells the name of something. **What is the title of your favorite book?**
3. If you show **excitement**, you are happy and want to do something very much.
   How do you show excitement when you go out to play?

Follow rules for writing.

All writers follow rules. In this section, you will find rules to help you with your writing.

Using Punctuation

Use punctuation marks to make your writing easier to read.

Period

Use a **period** after a telling sentence.

I like to read.

Use a **period** after an initial.

Susan B. Anthony

Use a **period** after an abbreviation.

Mr. Bell
Dr. Wolf

Question Mark

Use a **question mark** after an asking sentence.

> Where are my shoes?

Exclamation Point

Use an **exclamation point** after a word that shows excitement.

> Wow! Help!

Use an **exclamation point** after a sentence that shows strong feeling.

> My dog Coco has my shoe!

Comma

Commas keep words and numbers from running together.

Use a **comma** between the day and the year.

May 20, 2011

Use a **comma** after the greeting in a letter.

Dear Aunt Janie,

Use a **comma** after the closing in a letter.

Love,
Ryan

Use a **comma** after words in a series.

Today I played catch with Joe, Mike, and Ginny.

May 20, 2011 **Date**

Greeting

Dear Aunt Janie,

Thanks for the mitt. My dad and my brother throw balls to me. It is fun!

Closing

Love,

Ryan

P.S.

Today I played catch with Joe, Mike, and Ginny.

Apostrophe

Use an **apostrophe** to make a contraction.

Words		Contractions
I am	—	I'm
it is	—	it's
he is	—	he's
she is	—	she's
did not	—	didn't
do not	—	don't
is not	—	isn't
let us	—	let's

Using Capital Letters

When you follow the rules for writing, your reader can understand what you write. Here are the rules for using capital letters.

Capital Letters

Use a **capital letter** for the first word in a sentence.

The walrus has two big tusks.

Use a **capital letter** for the word **I**.

Yesterday I drew a walrus.

Capital Letters

Use a **capital letter** for names of people and places.

Rosa Parks Texas

Use a **capital letter** for name titles.

Dr. Seuss Ms. Lim
Mrs. Cooper Mr. Ford

Use **capital letters** for book titles.

I read the book My Five Senses.

Use a **capital letter** for holidays.

New Year's Day Labor Day
Thanksgiving Flag Day

Use a **capital letter** for the days of the week.

Sunday	Thursday
Monday	Friday
Tuesday	Saturday
Wednesday	

Use a **capital letter** for the months of the year.

January	May	September
February	June	October
March	July	November
April	August	December

Making Plurals

Plural means *more than one*. Add an **-s** to most nouns to make the plural.

Singular Nouns	Plural Nouns
book	books
pencil	pencils
teacher	teachers

Some nouns use a new word to make the plural.

Singular Nouns	Plural Nouns
child	children
foot	feet
man	men
woman	women

Checking Spelling

Always check your spelling when you write. Here is an ABC list of words you can use.

Aa

about	and	ask
all	are	at
am	as	away

Bb

be	blue	bus
big	brown	but
black	bug	by

Cc

call	can't	cold
came	car	color
can	circle	come

Dd

day	do	don't
did	does	down
didn't	dog	draw

Ee

each	eat	every
ear	eight	eye

Ff

face	first	four
feet	five	Friday
find	for	from

Gg

get	goes	great
give	good	green
go	gray	grow

Hh

had	have	here
hand	he	home
has	help	how

Ii

I	if	is
I'm	in	it

Jj

jar	job	jump
jelly	joke	just

Kk

keep	kitten	knew
kind	knee	know

Ll

last	let	live
left	like	long
leg	little	look

Mm

made	me	most
make	Monday	must
many	more	my

Nn

name	next	nose
need	nine	not
new	no	now

Oo

of	on	orange
off	one	our
old	or	out

Pp

paper	please	purple
people	pretty	push
play	pull	put

Qq

quack	quick	quit
question	quiet	quiz

Rr

rain	red	ring
ran	ride	round
read	right	run

Ss

said	say	she
Saturday	see	six
saw	seven	Sunday

Tt

ten	they	Thursday
that	this	Tuesday
the	three	two

Uu

under	up	us
until	upon	use

Vv

van	very	visit
vegetable	vet	voice

Ww

was	Wednesday	what
we	were	white

Xx

x-ray	fi<u>x</u>	si<u>x</u>
fa<u>x</u>	mi<u>x</u>	wa<u>x</u>

Yy

yawn	yellow	you
year	yes	your

Zz

zebra	zigzag	zoo
zero	zip	zoom

Using the Right Word

Some words sound alike, but they are spelled differently and mean different things. These words are called **homophones**.

ate Steve ate crackers for a snack.

eight I have eight blocks.

blew The wind blew my kite.

blue My blue pants are too small.

buy The girls buy seeds at the store.

by I live by a park.

dear I wrote "Dear Nana."

deer We saw a deer in the woods.

for This snack is for my brother.

four He is four years old.

hear I can hear music.

here Please come here.

its The bird flaps its wings.

it's It's cold outside.

know Do you know my name?

no "No, I don't," said Theo.

one I lost one sock.

won My team won the game.

read	I read a story to Maya.
red	My favorite ball is red and blue.
road	Many trucks are on the road.
rode	I rode the bus to school.
their	My dog ran to their house.
there	There are two books on the table.
they're	They're playing tag.
to	We went to Grandpa's house.
too	Can I play, too?
two	I had two eggs for breakfast.

Understanding Opposites

Opposites tell about ideas that are completely different from each other. Opposite words are called **antonyms**.

day	night
happy	sad
hot	cold
left	right
on	off
up	down

Understanding Sentences

A sentence tells a complete idea and has two parts.

Naming Part	+	Telling Part	=	Sentence
Marco	+	runs.	=	Marco runs.
Ty and I	+	play ball.	=	Ty and I play ball.

A sentence begins with a **capital letter**. It ends with a **period**, a **question mark**, or an **exclamation point**.

Capital Letters **End Marks**

The boys play basketball.

Does Paulo want to play, too?

He scores the first basket!

Subjects and Verbs That Agree

In every sentence, the subject must agree with the verb.

If the subject names one person, place, or thing, you usually add **-s** to the verb.

person	Vilay	laughs.
place	The store	opens.
thing	A snake	slithers.

If the subject names more than one person, place, or thing, do not add **-s** to the verb.

people	Vilay and Annie	laugh.
places	The stores	open.
things	Snakes	slither.

Different Kinds of Sentences

A **telling sentence** tells about something or someone. It ends with a **period**.

I like to play tag.

An **asking sentence** asks a question. It ends with a **question mark**.

Will you play with me?

An **exclamatory sentence** shows excitement or strong feelings. It ends with an **exclamation point**.

You are it!

Using the Parts of Speech

The words that you use in your writing are called the **parts of speech**.

Nouns

A **noun** is a word that names a person, place, or thing.

person:	boy	nurse
place:	home	school
thing:	book	chair

A **common noun** names any person, place, or thing. A **proper noun** names a specific person, place, or thing.

Common Nouns	Proper Nouns
girl	Julia
school	Grant School

Singular and Plural Nouns

A **singular noun** names one person, place, or thing. A **plural noun** names more than one person, place, or thing.

Singular Nouns	Plural Nouns
cat	cats
dog	dogs
bug	bugs
apple	apples
friend	friends

Pronouns

A **pronoun** is a word that takes the place of a noun.

Molly likes grapes.

She likes grapes.

(*She* takes the place of the noun **Molly**.)

Robert peeled a banana.

Robert peeled *it*.

(*It* takes the place of the noun **banana**.)

Common Pronouns

I	we	her	them
it	us	me	they
she	he	his	you

Verbs

A **verb** is a word that shows action or helps complete a thought.

Action Verb

The squirrel jumps from tree to tree.

Some Action Verbs

ask	hug	play
fix	go	race
help	jump	read

Linking Verb

The squirrel is a great jumper.

Some Linking Verbs

am	is	are	was
were	be	been	

Action-Verb Tenses

Some **action verbs** tell what is happening now, in the **present**.

Sam helps his mother.

Some **action verbs** tell what happened before, in the **past**. Verbs in the past tense usually end in **-ed**.

Sam helped his mother last night.

Present Tense	Past Tense
cook	cooked
mix	mixed
pull	pulled
walk	walked

Linking-Verb Tenses

Linking verbs can complete thoughts in the **present** or in the **past**. Instead of ending in **-ed**, a past-tense linking verb becomes a different word.

I am a first grader.
I was a kindergartner.

The children are happy.
The children were happy.

Present Tense	Past Tense
am	was
is	was
are	were

Adjectives

An **adjective** is a word that tells something about a noun.

Kiki is my silly cat.

(*Silly* tells **what kind** of cat.)

She has three spots.

(*Three* tells **how many** spots.)

An adjective can **compare two** people, places, or things.

Socks is faster than Kiki.

An adjective can **compare more than two** people, places, or things.

Socks is the fastest cat I know.

Editing and Proofreading Marks

You can use the marks below to make changes to your writing. Your teacher may also use these marks to help you improve your writing.

Mark	Meaning	Example	Edited
≡	Capitalize a letter.	Ezra Jack keats wrote Pet Show.	Ezra Jack Keats wrote Pet Show.
/	Make a capital letter lowercase.	Archie wanted to take the Cat.	Archie wanted to take the cat.
⊙	Add a period.	It was time to go, but the cat was missing ⊙	It was time to go, but the cat was missing.
℘	Take something out.	His friends ~~they~~ looked for the cat.	His friends looked for the cat.
∧	Add a letter, a word, or words.	They searched ∧ (here) and there.	They searched here and there.
? ∧ ∧ !	Insert punctuation.	Finally ∧ Archie's friends left for the show.	Finally, Archie's friends left for the show.
sp.	Correct the spelling error.	The endin (sp.) had some surprises.	The ending had some surprises.

Theme Words

In this section, you will find lists about people, places, and things. There are also word lists for animals, foods, and activities.

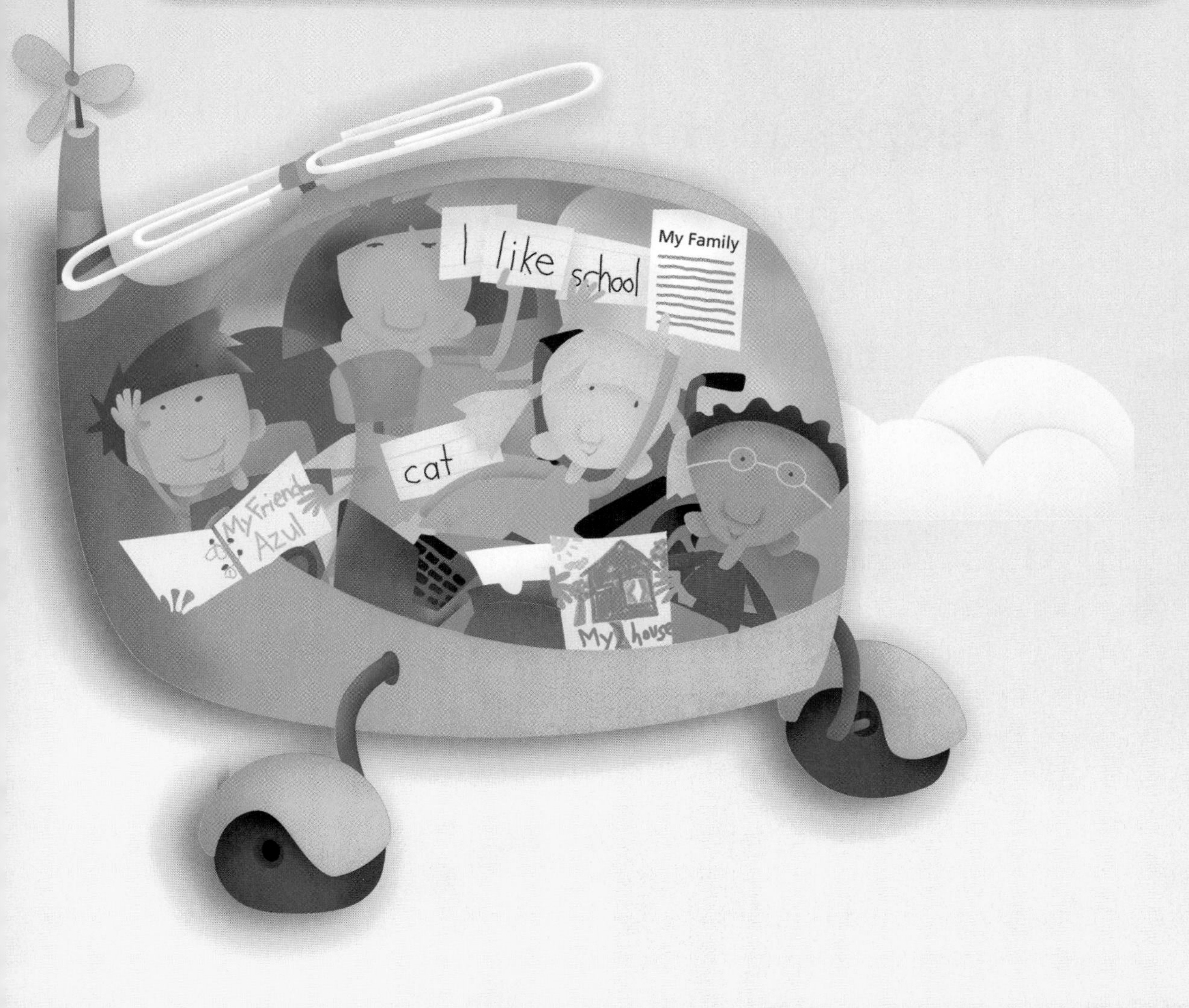

People

People live and work all around us.

People at Home

aunt
baby
brother
cousin
father
friend
grandma
grandpa
mother
sister
uncle

People at Work

doctor
nurse
pilot
police officer
truck driver

People at School

aide
bus driver
cook
custodian
secretary
teacher

Places

Going
places is fun!

A
B
C
D
farm
forest
field
river
island
park
highway
lake
road
city
bridge
beach
street
EXIT
55
40
25

Things

In your classroom centers, you may find interesting things.

Math

clock
coins
counters
rulers
scale
shapes

Art

brushes
clay
glue
paint
scissors

Science

fish
leaves
magnets
rocks
seeds
shells

Library

big books
dictionary
globe
little books
magazines
map

Writing

computer
crayons
journals
markers
paper
pencils

Music

CD's
drum
rhythm sticks
shakers

Animals

Animals live all over the world.

Rain Forest

ants
frog
monkey
parrot

Oceans

crab
fish
octopus
shark
starfish
stingray
whale

Desert

coyote
lizard
snake
spider

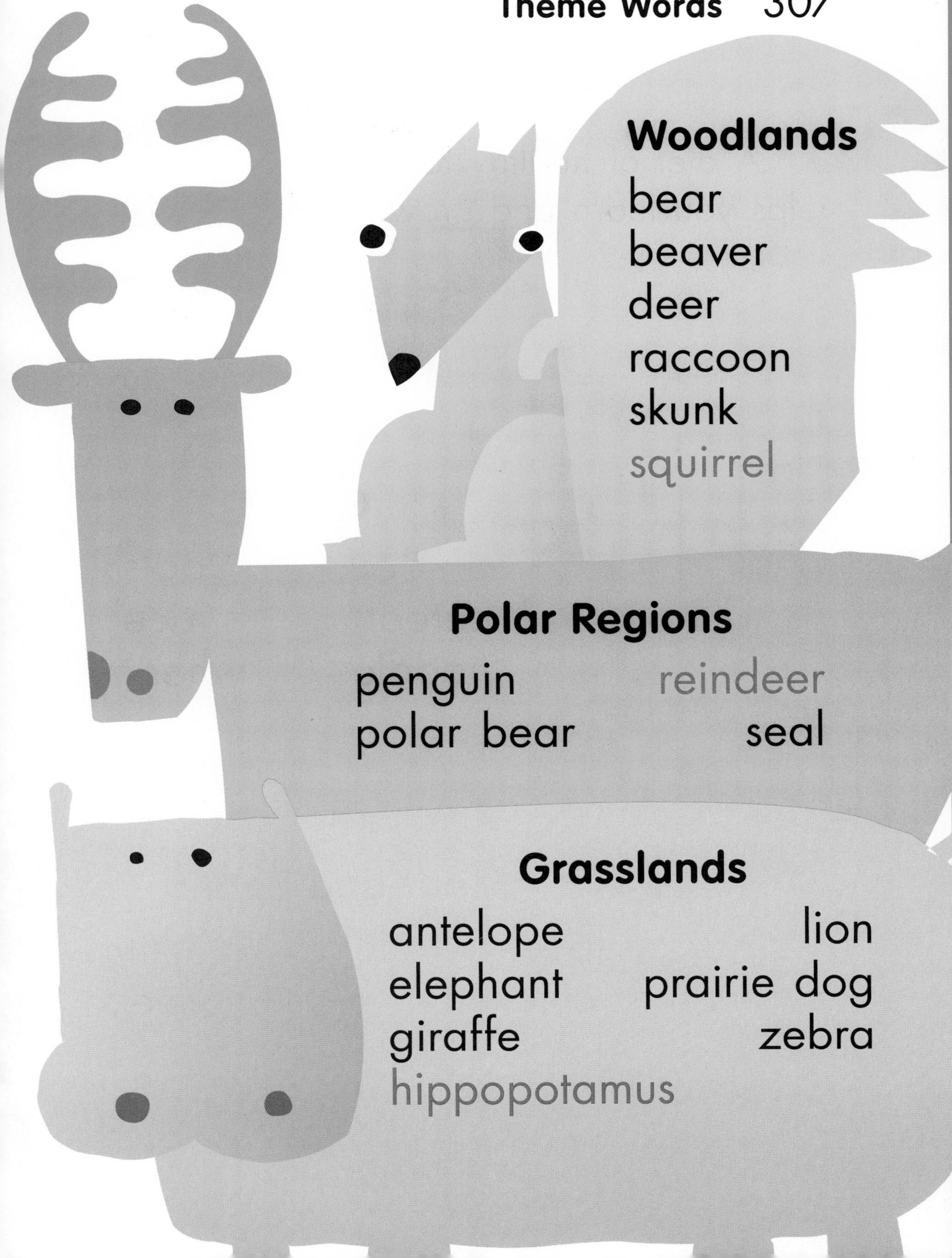

Woodlands

bear
beaver
deer
raccoon
skunk
squirrel

Polar Regions

penguin
polar bear
reindeer
seal

Grasslands

antelope
elephant
giraffe
hippopotamus
lion
prairie dog
zebra

Foods

A diet of healthy foods helps you learn and grow.

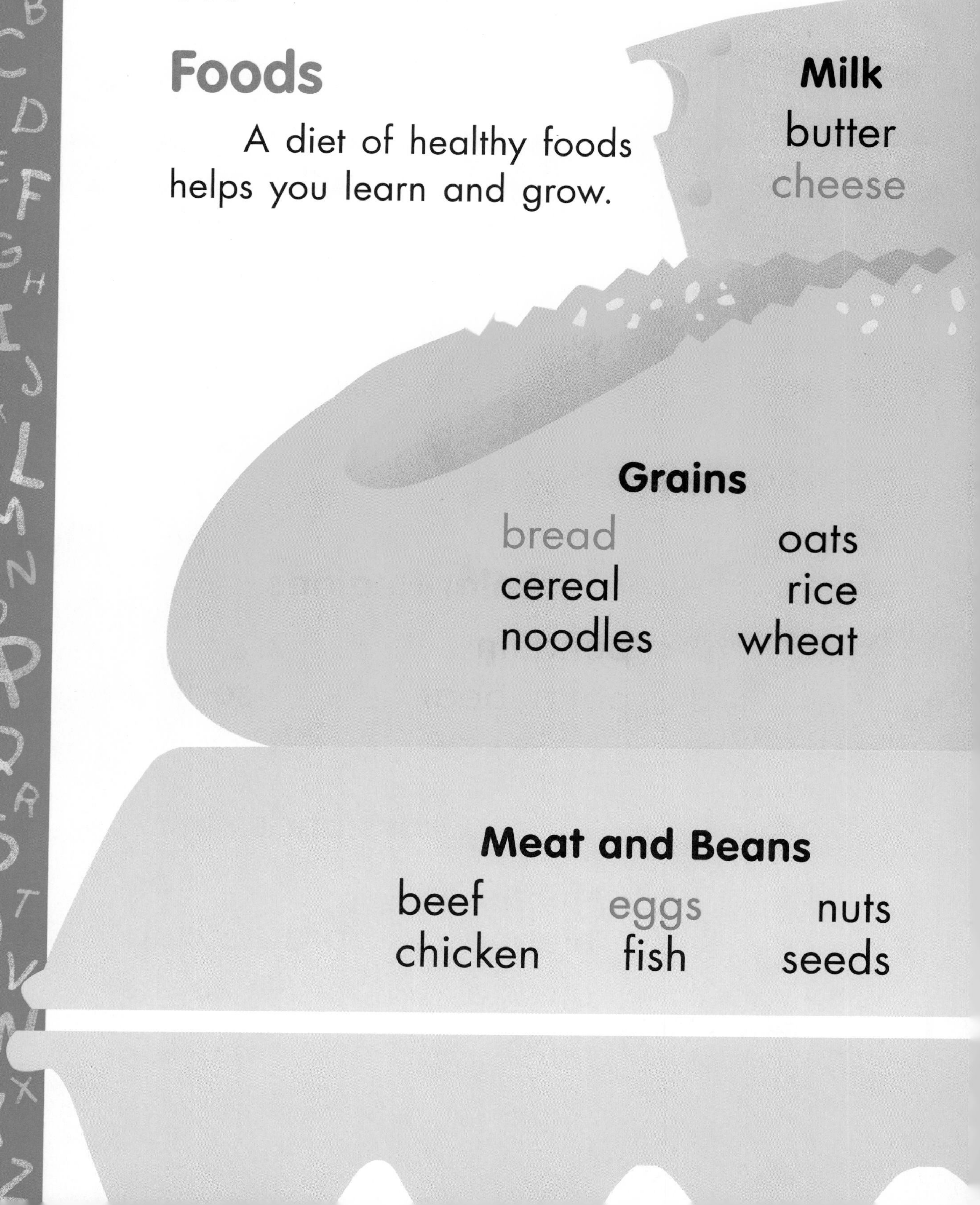

Milk

butter
cheese

Grains

bread
cereal
noodles
oats
rice
wheat

Meat and Beans

beef
chicken
eggs
fish
nuts
seeds

Vegetables

beans
carrots
celery
corn
peas
potatoes

Fruits

apple
banana
grapes
melon
orange
pear

Activities

What do you like to do at the park?

A B C
Welcome to
Green
Lake
Enjoy your day!
listen
watch
play
fly
fish
read
build

Credits

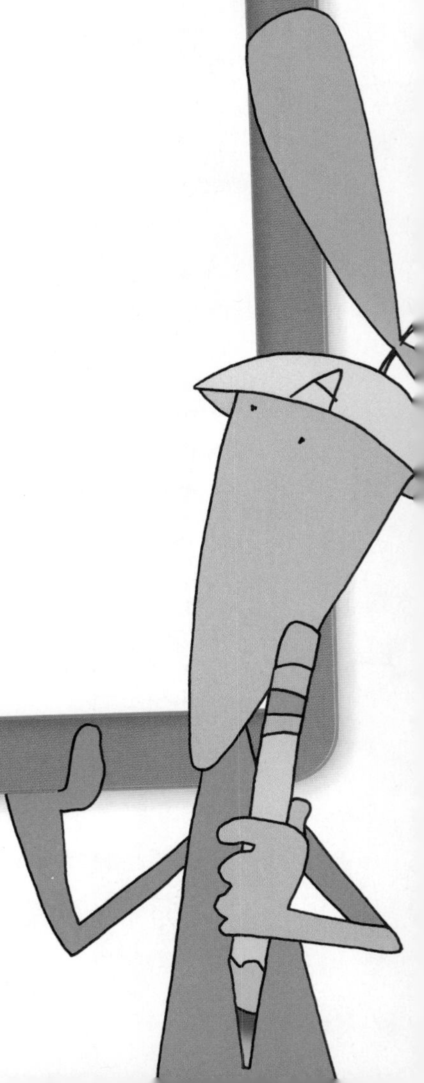

Index

The **index** will help you find information in this book. Let's say you want to write a letter. You can look in your index under *letters* for help.

A

B

C

K

L

M

N

O

P

T

U

V

W